From Slavery to Community Builder

Also by Charles Warren

Address Unknown

Also by Dr. Canter Brown, Jr.

Florida's Peace River Frontier
In the Midst of All That Makes Life Worth Living: Polk County, Florida, to 1940
Tampa in Civil War and Reconstruction
Tampa before the Civil War
Henry Bradley Plant: Gilded Age Dreams for Florida and a New South
Fort Meade, 1849-1900
Florida's Black Public Officials, 1867-1924
None Can Have Richer Memories: Polk County, Florida, 1940-2000
Family Records of the African American Pioneers of Tampa and Hillsborough County

From Slavery to Community Builder

The Story of Lawrence B. Brown

Charles Bruce Warren
Additional text by Canter Brown, Jr.
Foreword by Clifton P. Lewis

Neighborhood Improvement Corporation of Bartow, Inc.
Bartow, Florida 33830
2021

From Slavery to Community Builder: The Story of Lawrence B. Brown
Neighborhood Improvement Corporation of Bartow, Inc.

All rights Reserved.
Published 2021

Copyright © 2021 by Neighborhood Improvement Corporation of Bartow, Inc.

No part of this publication may be reproduced, stored in a retrieval system, or transmitted in any form or by any means electronic, mechanical, photocopying, recording, or otherwise, without the written permission of the Neighborhood Improvement Corporation of Bartow, Inc.

Manufactured in the United States of America
First Printing

ISBN: 978-0-578-99227-3 (Paperback Edition)
ISBN: 978-0-578-98031-7 (Hardcover Edition)
ISBN: 978-0-578-98036-2 (e-book Edition)

Library of Congress Control Number: 2021917994

Neighborhood Improvement Corporation of Bartow, Inc.
Bartow, FL 33830

For the many men and women who suffered the horrors of slavery and, when freed, in spite of obstacles and violence against them, had the grace to use their talents and skills to make our country a better place.

Contents

Figures ix

Foreword xiii

Preface xix

Acknowledgements xxi

Chapter 1 L. B. Brown Before Bartow by Canter Brown Jr. 1

Chapter 2 Lawrence Brown's Life in Bartow 19

Chapter 3 The L. B. Brown House/Museum 73

Chapter 4 The Neighborhood Improvement Corporation Rescues the Brown House/Museum 95

Chapter 5 A Search for Truth 111

Chapter 6 A Living Legacy 123

Notes 135

Index 143

Figures

1. Photo of railroad in Archer, Florida 2
2. Photo of busy rail-side "woodrack" in Archer, Florida 3
3. Alachua map 1880 5
4. Peter Brown called for jury duty 7
5. Political cartoon on election 8
6. Spring Garden, Florida 11
7. Uriah Mitchell Bennett 12
8. Marriage certificate of Brown and Elizabeth Washington 13
9. Spring Garden's business district 15
10. The passage of the railroad through Spring Garden, DeLeon Springs and Glenwood 17
11. Downtown Bartow 1885 19
12. Hallie Mae 21
13. Ledger page showing Brown's parcel of land in DeLeon Springs 23
14. Ledger page of Brown's land purchase in Polk County 24
15. Ledger page of Brown's agreement with Ben Knight 26
16. Ledger page with more of Ben Knight 28
17. Ledger page with more Ben Knight 30
18. Ledger page with final entry on Ben Knight 31
19. Ledger page with final payment to Milam 32
20. Ledger page haircut agreement 33
21. Ledger page showing renters' payments 34
22. Bartow's Main Street 37
23. Annie Belle Brown 39
24. Benjamin Burnett 40
25. List of Lawrence Brown's family 40
26. Ledger page showing business transactions 41
27. Louvenia Brown 44
28. Bartow celebration of completion of Polk County courthouse 44
29. Ledger page of peanut farm 46

30. Ledger page noting stolen shotgun 47
31. Ledger page on price of pork 48
32. Lorenzo Brown 49
33. Ledger page of a dream 50
34. Ledger page showing Annie's involvement 51
35. Eulogistic Services for Lawrence Clifford Brown 53
36. Mary Brown Tugerson 54
37. Phosphate mine workers 55
38. L. B. Brown's mother, Catherine 56
39. Anniebelle Brown 57
40. Robert E. L. Brown 59
41. 1930 United States Census 59
42. Robert Brown and Clifton Lewis 61
43. Lawrence Brown 63
44. Lawrence Brown's grave 64
45. Peter Brown's Homestead Certificate 65
46. Peter Brown's Final Affidavit of Homestead 66
47. Memorandum page from Brown's Bible 67
48. Memorandum page from Family Bible with father's last words 68
49. Births in Family Bible 69
50. Page from funeral service for Annie Bell Brown 70
51. Joseph Tugerson, Lawrence brown's grandson 71
52. Sidney Johnston and Ralph Gineau 75
53. Program from first African American Heritage Festival 78
54. Photos of first African American Heritage Festival 79 and 80
55. Brown House before restoration 80, 81
56. Brown House after restoration 81
57. Foundation stone and pine log of Brown House 82
58. Welcome sign to Brown House 83
59. Decorative wood inside Brown House 84
60. Family photos at entryway to house 85
61. House dining room 86
62. House sitting room 87
63. Display case in sitting room 88
64. Sitting room 89
65. Front sitting room 90
66. Master bedroom 91
67. Intricate detail on balcony 92

68. Rental house 93
69. Early NIC meeting 96
70. Mission statement 98
71. NIC Charter Members 99
72. Workers cleaning West Bartow 100
73. Discussing the restoration project 103
74. Cleaning West Bartow 105
75. Lewis leading organizational meeting 105
76. Jeff Hoch in organizational meeting 106
77. Sandy Sheets leading organizational meeting 106
78. Tour of West Bartow 107
79. Joe DeLegge in organizational meeting 107
80. Doug Leonard leading NIC retreat 108
81. Early NIC board members 108
82. Dr. Canter Brown and Dr. Larry Rivers 109
83. Polk County Wood Turners 109
84. Cover of *The Golden Way* 111
85. Title page of *The Golden Way* 112
86. Illustration from *The Golden Way* 113 to 121
87. L. B. Brown House 124
88. Program for Youth Leadership Awards 125
89. Program for L. B. Brown Heritage Festival 127
90. Great Floridian Plaque 128
91. Newspaper clipping announcing Smithsonian display 130
92. Brown exhibit at Smithsonian's National Museum 131
93. Newspaper clippings of USF using Brown in classroom 132

Foreword

Reflections about the man - Lawrence Bernard Brown or "Mr. LB"

These observations are based on discussions I've had with a number of elderly individuals who knew Lawrence B. Brown. Included among those eye-witnesses was Lawrence Brown's son Robert E. L. Brown, who was seventeen at the time of his father's death in 1941.

Sadly, all of these individuals are now deceased. What follows is a summary of my personal research into Lawrence Brown's life as well as my understanding of the comments offered by those who knew him.

Lawrence Bernard Brown was born in 1856 under the debilitating system of slavery. At the tender age of nine, he gained his freedom when slavery was abolished in 1865.

As we wind the clock forward toward the end of Mr. Brown's life in 1941 and evaluate his overall achievements, we can readily see he fits the essential definition of a "solid citizen."

Born under the zero-sum system of slavery and progressing into life without a formal education, Lawrence Brown confronted the challenges of life with two strikes against him.

Because of his lowly beginning, fairness dictates that his lifetime achievements should be measured against the formidable hardships he faced—no formal education, no possessions, born into slavery, and afterwards living in a racist society.

In spite of those obstacles, Lawrence Brown became a successful entrepreneur leaving deep and clear footprints by way of public records, personal ledger books, masonry pillars bearing his initials, personal artifacts, and of course his magnificent old homestead built in 1892.

Clearly, Lawrence Brown was not the only ex-slave who rose to prominence in his local community. Many pioneer freedmen and freedwomen helped build their communities, and we know some of the names: Andy Moore, Jack Longworth, Henry Macon, Lela Boykin, and others.

However, the legacy of L. B. Brown stands out largely because of the clear physical proof of his achievements.

Stories shared by eye-witnesses

Those who actually knew Lawrence Brown described him as being a big man. Mr. Brown stood around six-three or six-four, with a stout physique. He was said to be a soft-spoken man who selected his words carefully, and pronounced each syllable distinctly. Mr. "LB," as he was also called, expected his instructions to be followed. But, despite his stern nature, he was said to be kind-hearted and a good listener.

Described as being a generous man who did not flaunt his wealth, he dressed modestly and was a devout Christian who practiced his belief by helping his neighbors. He was among the founding members of the Mount Gilboa Missionary Baptist Church in the early 1890s where he served as church clerk until his death in 1941.

Interestingly, according to Robert, Brown's wife Annie Belle (sometimes spelled Anna Bell) did not join her husband's church; she was a member of the nearby Saint James African Methodist Episcopalian Church. She may have joined the Saint James Church along with her first husband, Ben Burnett, who died in 1906. However, Robert reported that his mom was not a frequent church-goer and attended her husband's church more often than her own.

Robert's paternal grandmother, Catherine, a Native American, died in 1923, the year before his birth in 1924. In spite of never having seen her, he felt as if he knew her because his dad often spoke of her. Lawrence referred to his mother as "Kate."

Robert recalled that contrary to all the fuss currently being made about his family, theirs was a normal family life. He did not feel special or better than his neighbors. His parents managed a normal household, and his mother's daily routine was fairly typical of most housewives. His father conducted business matters in the little shop that was located on the north side of the house.

Robert remembered his mother as being a devoted and loving woman who fussed about her children and husband. Whenever his parents walked together, his mom usually placed her hand in the crook of his dad's arm and walked slightly behind him; Annie Belle was careful never to contradict her husband or otherwise attempt to overshadow him. If there was any disagreement, they apparently resolved it away from the children. Theirs was a typical husband-wife relationship of that time in which the husband was the head of the family.

His dad spent a great deal of the family's wealth caring for his wife after she became ill following Robert's birth. Dr. Wilson, a prominent white doctor, attended to Annie Bell at the Brown's residence. Robert related that his father often drove his wife to the Clara Frye Clinic in Tampa. At times, her treatment required her spending several days living with relatives in Tampa. Annie Belle never fully recovered from Robert's birth. Her disability required her to use a wheelchair until her death in 1938.

Robert's memory of his mother's disability as a result of his birth continued to affect him even as an old man in his mid-seventies. As he shared this story with me, he wiped tears from his eyes. Robert concluded this painful story by saying softly, "I hurt my momma when I was born."

The only time Robert recalled his dad hitting him was when he disrespected his mother. At the young age of seven or eight, Robert approached his father in the yard and asked permission to do something that, by the time of the interview, he no longer remembered. His father directed him to "ask your momma," to which Robert replied "I did ask her, and she said no." His father instinctively lashed out with a buggy whip he was holding and "stung my little leg." He said he was wearing short pants and the sting really hurt. Lawrence Brown was highly protective of the women in the family; Robert does not recall ever disrespecting his mother again.

As Robert and I stood on the second-floor porch, he shared another lesson he was taught, this time by his mother. He was chatting a lot as eight-year-olds often do, when his mother directed his attention to a noisy old wagon as it moved along the dusty and rutted Second Avenue directly below. Sometime later, the wagon returned traveling in the opposite direction. His mother told him to "hush and listen to the wagon now." Robert replied, "I don't hear nothing now." His mother responded, "That's because the wagon is full now, it was empty the first time." Robert never forgot the lesson about "an empty wagon making a lot of noise." Annie Bell often taught her children important life lessons in this manner.

In response to my statement that we were thinking about placing a special marker, or historical markers, at the Evergreen Cemetery to direct tourists to the Brown family plot, Robert asked me to reconsider doing so because he believed that it might be seen as an attempt to elevate his family above others. He asked me to keep things in perspective.

Notwithstanding Robert's humility about his family, especially his father, there can be no doubt that L. B. Brown was highly respected among his neighbors, and throughout the broader community.

Although L. B. Brown's business activities were of benefit to the community, it is obvious that he and his family benefitted as well. "Mr. LB" was an entrepreneur who clearly understood the concept of supply and demand, how to meet those demands, and also how to manage his businesses. Houses sold and money loaned would accrue interest, usually eight percent. Mr. Brown's business activities yielded good profits and provided comfort for his family.

It has been estimated that toward the end of his life, Lawrence Brown was worth hundreds of thousands of dollars—measured by today's standards.

Restoration and Preservation

During 1999, at the beginning of our effort to preserve "The Historic L.B. Brown House Museum," the abandoned house was known as "Mrs. Thomas' house." That's the name given because of the well-known former school teacher who lived there for many decades. Mrs. Louvenia Catherine Brown Thomas (or L.C.B. Thomas) had been a beloved public-school teacher. If anyone in Bartow knew about the contributions or even the previous existence of Lawrence Brown, they did not make it known to us.

The involvement of Lawrence Brown came to light one day during one of Robert's early visits. As we strolled the grounds, Robert mentioned—almost as a side observation—that his father had built the house. By that time, as a result of researching the title, we knew that Lawrence Brown had been the owner, but nothing in those county or city records indicated that L. B. Brown actually built the house. Thanks to Robert's off-hand comment, we now know that the builder was Lawrence Brown.

I recall finding an unidentified photo that someone suggested was of Tom Burnett, a prominent black businessman who lived nearby. But fortunately, during one of Robert's early visits, he identified that photo as his father! Following this fortunate casual incident Robert proceeded to provide valuable insights about his entire family.

On one of his last visits to Bartow, Robert handed me an old suit case. When I looked inside, I was astonished to find the old family Bible, a very attractive gold and pearl umbrella handle, a complete old umbrella, and remnants of several old ledger books with handwritten entries made by Lawrence Brown dating back to the 1890s. The writing on those deteriorated ledger pages provided clear evidence attesting to the "lost" legacy of Lawrence B. Brown.

I also remember a visit by Robert when he surprised me with a check for $5,000.00 to help with the restoration work. This amount combined with other donations was sufficient to make some repairs, but was not enough to repair the beautiful old gingerbread trim that gave the old house its unique Victorian look. Robert and I along with several others, including a minister from a nearby church, decided to stand in a circle and pray for help with the repairs of the gingerbread trim.

Just as Reverend Lawrence Moore, pastor of the nearby Burkett Chapple Primitive Baptist Church, finished praying for assistance and said "Amen," a white van drove up near where we were standing and five or six elderly white gentlemen stepped out. Much to my amazement, the leader of the group said they were retired wood-workers, and asked if we would allow them to help restore the ginger bread for which we had just prayed—free of charge! The irony and the timing of this offer almost overwhelmed me, and real tears rolled down my face. I was momentarily speechless as I contemplated what seemed to be a miracle. Someone in their group asked if I was OK. Of course, he had no way of knowing that his group had been the answer to our prayer.

The inspiring story of L.B. Brown is a compelling one and should be preserved and shared. The writer, Mr. Charles Warren, has done an outstanding job of telling the story of Lawrence Bernard Brown and the Historic L. B. Brown House. Hopefully, the readers will appreciate it as much as I do.

Clifton Lewis,
Founder of the LB Brown Preservation Project
June 2021

Preface

The Lawrence Brown story is important not just to Central Florida, but also to our nation. His story is an example of the contributions formerly enslaved people made to enrich their communities and ultimately, this country. Brown's efforts to build houses for workers and their families moving into the growing Bartow area was a key factor in helping to provide them with a decent standard of living and the opportunity for home ownership—an opportunity still denied many minorities and low-income families today.

I was fortunate to have Dr. Canter Brown, Jr. lend his expertise to the development of this book. The benefit of his writing skill, his knowledge of history and his familiarity with Central Florida cannot be overstated. His research proficiency proved valuable in writing the first chapter of this book as he uncovered new information about Lawrence Brown. His authorship of numerous books pertaining to Central Florida, enabled him to understand the dynamics of the times and environment during the early years of Brown's life.

Personal items found in the Brown home provided insight into his thoughts and character. These included Brown's own business Ledger and his annotated copy of the book, *The Golden Way*, published in 1898, which provided a roadmap to success during that time. Brown's notations and other markings of specific passages help us to understand him as a person.

The house he built to raise his family is, of course, an important part of this narrative. It is, after all, the most visible testament to his life. The story of how the house was saved through the efforts of Clifton Lewis and the Neighborhood Improvement Corporation of Bartow, Inc. (NIC) serve as an inspiration for others who aspire to like-minded projects. The NIC began as an organization engaging communities in bettering their neighborhoods and evolved into an organization responsible for saving a piece of important local history. The NIC continues working to keep the legacy of L. B. Brown and his historic house alive.

Lawrence Brown was a skilled craftsman and took pride in building a home with intricate displays of woodwork. Chapter Three is full of photographs which showcase his handiwork. Some of the most remarkable photographs are those showing the house prior to restoration compared to those post restoration. From the patterns of woodworking on the balcony to the mirrors and baseboards, the home is impressive and provides visitors a fun place to indulge their curiosity of the past.

The last chapter details L. B. Brown's Living Legacy. The impact Brown has had on Bartow and much of Central Florida is undeniable. He appears to have been a humble man who served his community and neighborhood with generosity and caring. Had Lawrence Brown's story remained untold, we would have lost an important historical account of one man's achievements. That this man was born into slavery, prospered through difficult and dangerous times for black men and women, and contributed significantly to his community, compels his story to be told.

My decision to write this book is propelled by the importance of Lawrence Brown's legacy and history. I came to realize how fragile and easily forgotten history can be. Brown's story needs to be preserved for future generations, for the students who will become our leaders and decisionmakers. Brown's values and ethics can be guideposts for how to live and how to lead.

My thoughts also go to the myriad of people who tour Lawrence Brown's home and have the intimate, up close and personal experience of hearing his story, as told through the knowledge and passion of Clifton Lewis. How much of that information is retained after their departure from Brown's home is not known. Sadly, stories of African American leaders and entrepreneurs are seldom part of school history books, leaving students to grow up without learning of the successes and contributions these men and women have made to our communities and nation.

It is my hope and intent that this book provides a tangible memory for visitors touring his home, providing them a written archive to share with their children, family, and friends for generations to come.

All proceeds from the sale of this book go directly to the Brown House Museum towards its maintenance and future needs. By purchasing this book, your important contribution keeps L. B. Brown's legacy alive.

Thank you.

Acknowledgements

There would be no L. B. Brown House/Museum standing today without the actions of Clifton Lewis. Thanks to his efforts, it was not demolished years ago. I am indebted to Clifton for taking the time to read my manuscript and offer many valuable insights. He also wrote the Foreword to this book which provides the reader with the story of how saving and restoring the Brown House took place.

Author and historian, Dr. Canter Brown, was gracious enough to read my manuscript and offer a number of helpful suggestions both regarding historical facts and writing style. He also researched and wrote the first chapter of this book. Dr. Brown is the author of *Florida's Peace River Frontier* and *In the Midst of All That Makes Life Worth Living: Polk County, Florida, to 1940*, along with a number of other historical works.

To my wife, Bernie, for her continued support and encouragement and for patiently editing early drafts.

Thanks to Lizzie Robinson-Jenkins, President of the Real Rosewood, Inc. for spending the better part of a day driving Clifton Lewis and myself around Alachua County in search of property locations to find the Peter Brown homestead.

Jean Reynolds, retired professor of English, and author of nine books at last count, for her helpful ideas regarding marketing, and her willingness to lend her knowledge and talent so graciously to help me through a myriad of publishing and other questions.

Thanks to Elijah Armstrong, Patricia Smith-Fields, and Barbara Fite for reading a draft of the book and offering their insightful suggestions.

Lois Murphy at the Polk County History Center for her support and help with photos in the Center's archives.

Thanks to Anna Holloway for her editing expertise and for being so responsive to my questions.

Shane Kent, Deputy Clerk at the Records Center in the Polk County Courthouse, for taking care to make good copies of old records.

I appreciate friends Karen White and Dorothy Lemmey being willing to read and offer their critique of various parts of this production.

Thanks to Stephanee Killen of Integrative Ink for her patience and helpful insights.

I appreciate Shay Cook for her time in helping to edit portions of this book.

I am grateful to all those talented people cited above for helping the story of L. B. Brown come to life.

Chapter 1

L. B. Brown Before Bartow

by Canter Brown, Jr.

Although Lawrence Bernard Brown and his construction in the 1890s of the beautiful L. B. Brown house are linked in our consciousness with the city of Bartow, Florida, his origins were decades earlier in frontier Alachua County in the midst of a sweltering summer and the state's final Seminole Indian war. Lawrence's slave parents Peter and Catherine Brown had been relocated from Georgia in late 1855 or early 1856 with at least three children. The Third Seminole or Billy Bowlegs War had erupted in December 1855, and the timing of their arrival in Florida hints that their owner acted from a sense of urgency to begin life anew. Whatever the specific cause that drove him, the owner chose to make his new start at a location—then called Wacahoota or Deer Hammock—that lay fifteen miles or so southwest of Gainesville. A local historian acknowledged that it amounted to "a crude, impoverished place." Rutted sand roads offered the only means of access to what optimistic settlers hoped eventually would become a prosperous agricultural center. In 1856, though, fears of Indian attack pervaded the vicinity, especially after June when word spread of violent deaths in a family—a tragedy that included children—that lived to the south of Wacahoota in today's Pasco County. Through these months of dislocation and war, a pregnant Catherine Brown meanwhile anticipated the birth of her next child. Baby Lawrence arrived on September 12th.[1]

The reason that Wacahoota managed to attract settlers in the mid-1850s was connected to the expected arrival of a railroad, a development that would open the region to commerce by affording dependable transportation at reasonable prices. Unfortunately, a host of problems—including the Seminole War—plagued the project and caused innumerable delays. Anxious local residents could only bide their time until the Florida Railroad's tracks reached the vicinity and a depot was opened. That event took until 1859. The moment when it ultimately occurred demanded a proper celebration as it turned out, one that took the form of a community barbecue on July 14th. Four hundred passengers rode in from Gainesville to participate along with nearly 1,000 others "who had come in from miles around." Euphoria ruled the day and cushioned the surprise announcement by company officials that they arbitrarily were naming the depot and community "Archer Station" to honor recently deceased railroad supporter and former Florida Secretary of State James T. Archer. Despite the Archer depot opening, construction crews then required eleven more months before the rails connected the Atlantic Ocean with the Gulf of Mexico. Finally, on June 13, 1860, a train could run 154 miles from Fernandina through Archer to Cedar Key (then, Cedar Keys).[2]

As suggested by this late-19th century image, trains and railroad affairs generally breathed life into the Archer economy following the opening of the Florida Railroad in 1859. (Collection of the author.)

Although he was too young at the time to remember these events, they remained important to Lawrence, nonetheless. The prewar developments established indelibly in the adolescent and adult the importance of rail transportation and impressed him with the opportunities that arose in Florida even for slaves and former slaves out of employment maintaining and operating railroads and associated businesses. Not only did railroads provide steady jobs and reasonable wage rates for work on trains and at depots, they also required staffing for a host of related concerns such as woodlots (sometimes called woodracks) and warehouses. In fact, Archer emerged as a center for warehousing area goods and products much as would Bartow in the 1880s. Even as a child, Brown would have noticed how very busy locales adjacent to railroad facilities tended to become and also how people desired to live close to their work. He would have gleaned, as well, the truth that some local residents enjoyed benefits of prosperity from taking advantage of those facts.[3]

Archer's busy rail-side "woodrack" offered a sight with which Lawrence Brown became intimately familiar in his youth. (Collection of the author.)

Until about his tenth birthday, so far as is known, Lawrence's life progressed without major incident at a measured pace typical for a slave child in that region of Florida during the late 1850s and early 1860s. The Archer area escaped violence and destruction during the Civil War despite the seizure of Cedar Key by United States troops in 1862, subsequent Union raids into Confederate-held territory, and a serious clash at Gainesville in August 1864. A brief flurry of activity at Archer surrounded the war's end in May 1865 when funds from the Confederate treasury ended up on the area plantation of former United States Senator David Levy Yulee. Black Federal troops came calling to commandeer the contraband, and it seems likely that, if they had not learned before, Peter Brown's family learned then of emancipation through word spread by those troopers.[4]

Still, the life of any child or adult slave offered trials that had to be endured, and this was true for Lawrence and his family members as well as for others. The comfort of faith and religion aided many. As Florida historian Larry Eugene Rivers concludes, "Religion served as a foundation for the triumph of shackled Africans and their descendants over spiritual and physical slavery." When it came to the Brown family, father Peter—despite being unable to read or write—enjoyed the reputation of being a "plantation minister" who likely performed his religious duties under the supervision of the Methodist Episcopal Church, South. After years of occasional visits by denominational representatives, in 1859, Archer finally gained an established Methodist congregation. Soon after secession two years later, however, the minister withdrew to accompany area troops into the Confederate Army and left the local church rudderless. In the years that followed, slave members slowly withdrew. By the time peace came and attempts were made to revive the church, virtually no black members remained.[5]

Just as faith and religion aided the Browns during slavery, so, too, did they find comfort and encouragement in their religious ties during the early years of freedom. If Archer-area black Methodists functioned as did similar congregations located elsewhere in the state, they at first met in a brush arbor or log cabin under the preaching of a local minister such as Peter Brown. That situation changed in 1867 with the arrival of Rev. Jackson Welch of the Methodist Episcopal (or Northern Methodist) Church. Within one year, 136 black men, women, and children, including Brown family members, had joined the white pastor's congregation and helped him to open and maintain a sanctuary valued at the considerable sum of $800. More growth followed, but in 1870 the denomination transferred Welch elsewhere and temporarily left his local pulpit vacant.[6]

After a brief interim, a new minister—Lymus A. Anders—eventually reached the town, and his arrival heralded profound change for Archer and the Brown family. Described as "a full-blooded African," Anders had lifted himself from slavery, learned to read and write, and reached ordination in the crucible of Civil War-era Port Royal, South Carolina. White missionary teachers there had called him a "black Yankee" and saw him as "a man who led all the others of his race in enterprise and ambition." In Alachua County, Anders quickly encountered Francis B. Carolina, who had been assigned by the African Methodist Episcopal (AME) Church to spearhead the denomination's missionary work within the county. Their attachment grew to the point that the Archer pastor soon opted to unite with Carolina's ministry. "He joined our church in the latter part of 1870 bringing in about [160] or more of the members from the [Northern Methodist] Church," an AME official recorded. "He was their pastor, and they loved him; and as such they continued to follow him until through his influence the Churches on the Archer mission were made strong enough to support their own pastor. Brother Anders joined our Conference at Madison on the 12th day of December." A few weeks earlier, already acting on behalf of the AME Church, Anders had presided at the Archer marriage of 14-year-old Lawrence's brother Gilbert to "Miss Tempe Howard."[7]

In Anders's conversion lay the origins of Archer's Mt. Pisgah AME Church with which the Browns and young Lawrence came to associate closely. Located initially in a "log house" a short distance south of town, the church lay in close proximity to the Brown home and farm located a mile or so below. Father Peter over time assumed leadership roles within the congregation. Given the dynamic personalities often physically present on the denomination's behalf and the church's then-powerful role in Florida political and governmental affairs, the attraction for Peter is easily understandable. Of especial importance was the outsized influence of Presiding Elder Thomas Warren Long. A one-time Florida slave who had fought in the Union Army and founded public schools for black children in Madison County, he would claim a state senate seat representing Marion County in 1873 that he would hold for the rest of the decade.[8]

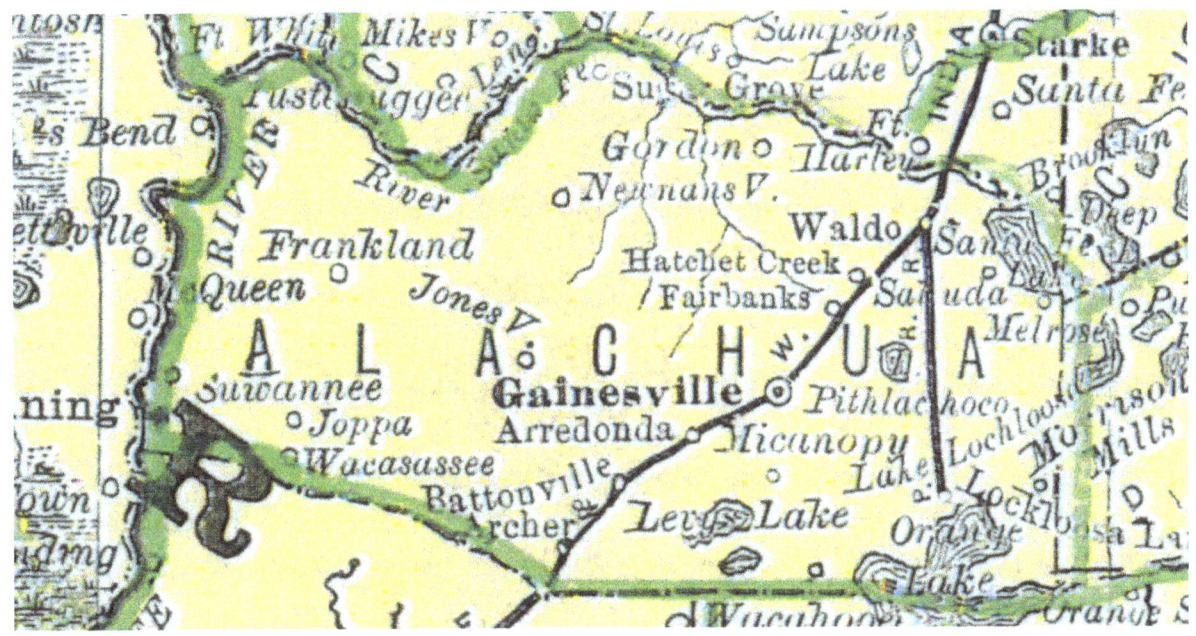

This 1880 map of Alachua County, Florida, helps to locate Peter and Catherine Brown's homestead and farm just south of Archer, itself situated southwest of Gainesville, Arredonda, and Battonville. (From Leslie's New World Atlas.*)*

Presiding Elder Long's impact upon the Mt. Pisgah congregation, Peter Brown, and his son Lawrence resounded most profoundly in the church's early years of existence. Long visited frequently. "What filled my heart with joy was that which happened on Sunday, the 26th of March, 1871," he reported in spring of that year regarding one such experience. "At Archer Mission, under the pastoral charge of Rev. Lymus Anders: During the quarterly meeting, I opened the doors for volunteers; and as I did so, I saw a weary old lady coming to join the Church. She looked to be about sixty years of age. She asked me if this was the same African M. E. Church which was established in Charleston thirty-nine or forty years ago; of which Morris Brown was bishop. She said she was a member of the A. M. E. Church in Charleston at that time and if this was the same African Church, she was compelled to come home to her first

5

love. I told her it was the same. She joined our church, and is now marching with us to battle against the wiles of Satan."[9]

One month later, Mt. Pisgah—presumably including Peter and, perhaps, Lawrence—rushed to Long's side at a moment special to the AME advent in Alachua. "On April 1st, I left Jacksonville, for Gainesville, arriving there on the 8th, where I met Rev. Lym[us Anders, with a large number of his members from Archer," Long recorded. "The people rallied in full force to see something they had never seen before; that is the corner stone of the A. M. E. Church in Gainesville; also the Rev. Francis Carolina, stationed pastor at Gainesville, was ready to have the corner stone of the church laid, which was done. This is something to be admired, when, it is to be remembered that, two years ago, one of the ministers of the M. E. church (North) said to one of our ministers, that no African church should be built in that city. His name is Isaac Davis. He had rather have a driver, than to serve God under His own vine and fig-tree."[10]

As Long's personal history suggested, Florida's AME Church in the late 1860s and into the 1870s perceived its mission to be broad in scope. Its fathers urged a dynamic presence in the affairs of state and asserted strong stands in terms of freedmen's rights, public education, social services, and other concerns. Its ministers and lay leaders had played important roles in rewriting Florida's constitution pursuant to the enactment in spring 1867 of what has been called Congressional or Military Reconstruction. This development had come in the wake of violent attacks on black leaders and one-time Unionists so severe that Alachua County, among others, had been placed under martial law in spring 1866. Thanks in part to AME leadership and the granting of voting rights to adult, male African Americans, Florida had elected its first black officials in late 1867. Among them, Union Army veteran Josiah T. Walls of Alachua County had claimed a seat in the constitutional convention and, in 1868, the state senate. By 1871 Walls labored in the nation's capital as a member of the United States House of Representatives.[11]

As black war veteran and fellow Alachua Countian Walls trod Congressional hallways on their behalf during the early 1870s, a growing Brown family slowly marked progress in building a secure life for itself. Peter farmed, having homesteaded thirty-nine acres. The children, including Lawrence, assisted as was typical for the time. Peter and Catherine, on the other hand, determined that their young son also would gain a suitable education. The Northern Methodists likely had operated a school in the first years of its local presence; but in 1869, Florida authorized a public-school system. AME representation in the state legislature had propelled the measure toward adoption, and, when a school opened at Archer within a year or two, Lawrence was counted as one of the pupils. The first classes could well have convened at Mt. Pisgah Church.[12]

The Archer vicinity began to prosper in the 1870s by weaning its economy away from dependence on cotton production, and this benefited the Browns immensely. The availability of rail transportation factored heavily in the change by allowing a shift toward truck farming and the growing of perishable fruits and vegetables. As a local man explained in May 1872:

"Business is very good at this season and the planters, with one or two exceptions, are boasting of their crops and are in excellent spirits. About fifty crates of cucumbers are shipped from here daily to Savannah and other cities. Large crops of melons have been planted and promise a good return. The writer saw one several days since nearly ripe enough to pluck. Corn is silking. We also have had and still have plenty of Irish potatoes, beans, green peas, &c." Archer meanwhile had grown considerably and, according to the local man, now boasted "two fine hotels, good water, good society and a hearty welcome to strangers." He added, "There are six stores here doing a very good business and one in erection, nearly complete." The man closed by noting: "There are also two colored churches here and an academy for the instruction of colored children. We have had until recently two schools, free, but they closed in the last week for the summer months."[13]

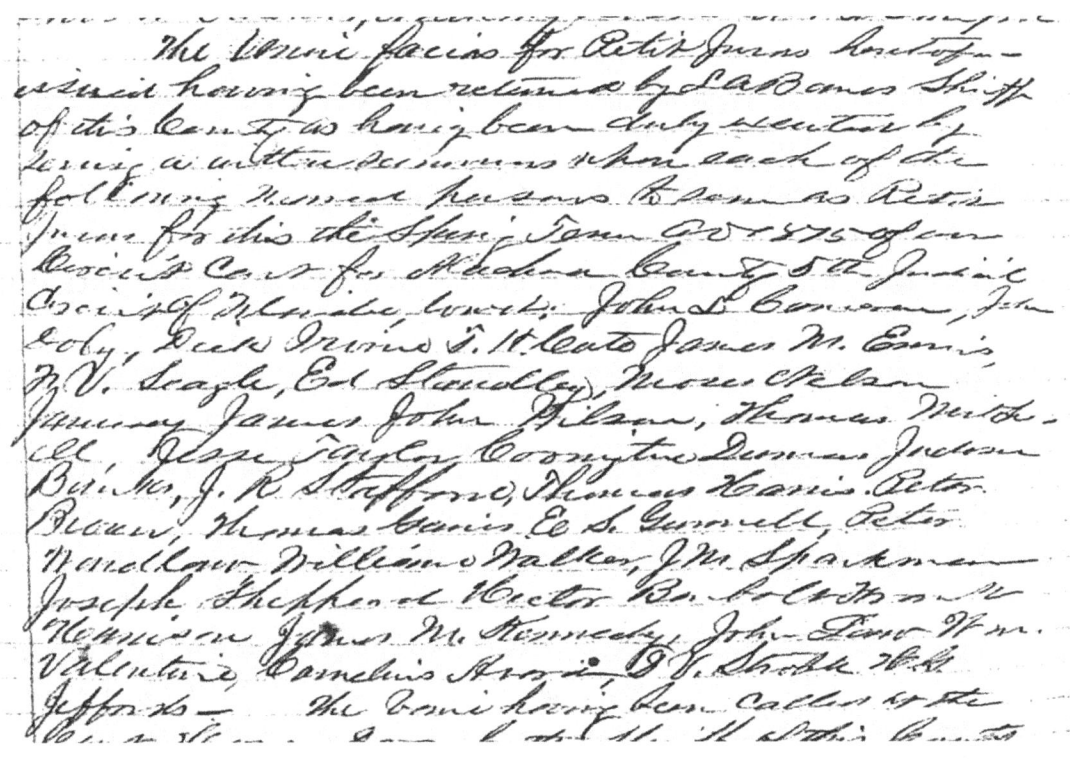

L. B. Brown's father Peter Brown in the 1870s began to advance in Alachua County Republican Party politics. One reward came in spring 1875 when, as illustrated by this excerpt from surviving county records, he was called for jury duty. (From Judgment Record C, Alachua County Clerk of Court, Gainesville.)

Unfortunately, Archer's "good society" and "hearty welcome" faltered in the face of an implacable racial and political divide. Most area black men such as Peter Brown voted the Republican ticket, whereas most whites backed the Democrats. Many participants perceived elections literally in terms of survival. For freedmen, the possibility of white victories held out the likelihood of a return to slavery in all but name. Florida precedent suggested as much, reflecting back to legislative actions in 1865 and 1866—before participation by black voters—when the legislature adopted infamous "black codes" to replace outdated "slave codes." Biennial voting contests accordingly spawned occasional violence, often sparked threats of economic reprisals, and prompted charges and countercharges of election fraud and voter intimidation. The nation heard of incidents at Archer during the 1874 general election. "A negro named Landers, together with several hundred of his followers," the Democratic *Savannah Morning News* alleged that November, "took possession of the polls, and negroes were allowed to vote whether they were entitled to do so or not."[14]

The facts of the 1874 general election at Archer remain murky, but, whatever occurred, Peter Brown likely participated. Had it not been for a family tragedy, his son Gilbert probably would have stood by his side. Unfortunately, earlier in the year Gilbert had died. The single reference to the event indicated that the young man had "burned," although the context hinted at a house fire in which Gilbert's wife and child or children also perished. Whether the calamity resulted from political activity cannot be confirmed from the surviving record. Yet, the possibility of a political connection cannot be discounted entirely.[15]

The events of 1874, as it happened, served as prelude for Peter and Lawrence for the general election two years later. The year 1876 marked the nation's centennial, but in Florida it stood out more in the minds of Republicans for the threat of a Democratic takeover of state government. Events subsequently occurring at Archer Precinct No. 2, ones involving both men, set the stage for national scandal. As may have occurred in 1874, local Republican leaders rallied black voters to ensure maximum tallies for their candidates. In practical terms, this meant that 200 or more Republican ballots were cast than registration lists would have allowed. Peter was registered and voted. Lawrence, ineligible at age twenty, also voted. Resulting charges of "Archer Election Frauds" rocked the nation. The news took on outsized importance because the results affected not only the election of Florida's governor but also that of the president of the United States. Compromise eventually ruled the day. While Democrat George F. Drew claimed the state's executive office, the heralded "Compromise of 1877" ushered Republican Rutherford B. Hayes into the White House.[16]

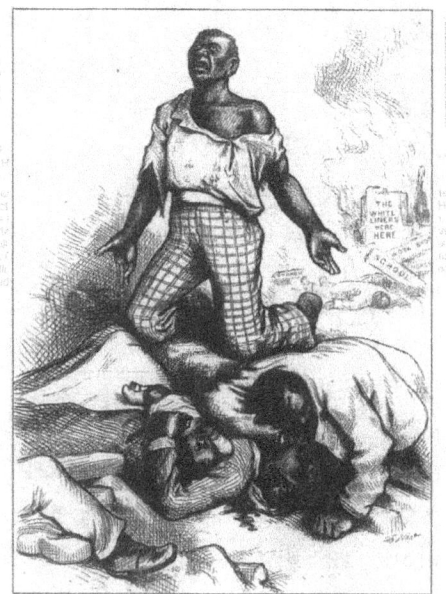

Famed cartoonist Thomas Nast portrayed the deep fears harbored by many freedmen and their families that a Democratic Party victory in November 1876 elections might lead to a return to slavery in all but name. (From Harper's Weekly, *September 2, 1876.)*

The story did not end there. Congressional and other investigators quickly spread out following the 1876 election to discover the reality of what had happened. United States senators learned of Lawrence's involvement as early as January 8, 1877. Published testimony of hearings held at Gainesville highlighted his role:

Lawrence Brown sworn and examined.
By the Chairman [Aaron A. Sargent, of California:

Question. Where did you vote on election day?—Answer. Archer.
Q. What box?—A. No. 2.
Q. What ticket?—A. Republican.

By Senator [Henry Cooper [of Tennessee:

Q. Lawrence Brown, you say?—A. Yes, sir.
Q. You voted the Republican ticket?—A. Republican ticket.[17]

Peter, Lawrence, and the rest of the Brown family managed at first to avoid repercussions from the events that took place at Precinct No. 2 despite Democratic takeover of state and county government in 1877. Republicans initially denied committing fraud, and sufficient evidence of improper Democratic conduct and intimidation elsewhere in the state deflected attention from Archer. In the aftermath of Lawrence's 21st birthday on September 12, 1877, Peter somewhat surprisingly even found himself relied upon as a witness in a local criminal proceeding. That state of affairs, unfortunately for the Browns, abruptly changed in April 1878. The sudden and detailed admission of the frauds by white Alachua Republican leader Leonard G. Dennis astounded the state and nation. The "startling developments" produced a political firestorm. At Archer, the Browns quickly found themselves in the midst of an untenable personal situation, threatened indirectly if not directly by angry Democrats and fearfully uncertain of their safety.[18]

Thus, by mid-1878, Lawrence Brown possessed ample reason to seek a safe haven elsewhere than in Alachua County, one free of political troubles that offered day-to-day employment coupled with the promise of future opportunity. In the circumstances, he left his family at Archer to relocate to a region reminiscent in its frontier remoteness to that of Wacahoota two decades earlier. Although the Spring Garden area of Volusia County lay near the St. Johns River, the area's distance from that navigable stream when coupled with the nature of the region severely limited access. "We entered, and at once plunged into a Tropical jungle," a visitor explained. "This is a remarkable feature of Florida—the distinctly-marked division between the character of the soil and vegetation. We might, as far as appearances were concerned, have been a few minutes before in the pine-woods of New England; but here was a wild revel of Tropic luxuriance. The lofty live-oak, with its sombre drapery of moss; the graceful palmetto, with its crown of foliage; the beautiful magnolia, with its shining leaves glimmering through the forest-gloom; the vines, like huge serpents, twisting in and out of all this luxuriance; the delicate yellow jessamine sparkling with stray beams of sunshine—these are the characteristics of the hammock-lands of Florida."[19]

In 1878, no railroad approached near to Spring Garden; but the vicinity boasted other assets that appealed to Lawrence Brown besides its remoteness. Particularly, most of the principal settlers were Northerners who spent winter seasons in Florida before returning to Illinois, New York, or elsewhere for the remainder of each year. Many, but not all, were Republicans who welcomed black workers. They had underscored their attitude toward freedmen in early 1878 when a series of violent incidents had prompted them to appeal for Federal assistance when local authorities would not act. A dispatch from Washington, DC, dated March 15, explained: "The owners of extensive orange-groves in Spring Garden, Fla., who were formerly of Illinois, and are friends of Senators [Richard James Oglesby, of Illinois, and [Henry Davis, of West Virginia, have written to the agent of the Government asking him to lay before these Senators facts growing out of the murder of a number of their colored help, in order that the Federal Government may take action. These orange-planters, failing to secure white help, employed negroes. This so enraged the 'Crackers'—a disturbing element of Florida—that they commenced warfare against the negroes, asserting that none of that race should be employed in that country. The result of the conflict was the murder of several negroes. The Sheriff of the county refuses to make arrests. Affidavits and the papers at the Coroner's inquest have been submitted to the authorities here. The murders took place six weeks ago."[20]

Lawrence may well have read coverage of the Volusia murders and efforts to afford security to the few black workers who remained, as well of the relatively benevolent attitudes of Spring Garden's principal families. What was more, he likely learned from the *Florida Agriculturalist*, a newspaper published at the new town of DeLand located about five miles south of Spring Garden, that leading area investors were expanding operations in 1878. Until that point, the rural community's principal backer had been George H. Norris of Illinois, who had arrived on the scene six years earlier. Norris had secured an old colonial grant of over 7,000 acres situated three miles south of beautiful Spring Garden Springs (now DeLeon Springs State Park) and begun laying out orange groves. He also set about hacking from the landscape "a broad sandy lane" over five miles in length. Beginning in fall 1872, the developer had marketed 50-acre tracts that branched off his "Grand Avenue." Progress came slowly; but by late 1877, Norris had expanded his road grid and could count 20 families that had taken advantage of his entrepreneurial initiatives. This offered sufficient encouragement for him to open in 1878 a shallow-draft steamer connection with the St. Johns River through Spring Garden Lake and to erect a citrus packing house on the lake's shores. Another man contributed a saw-mill. Yet another opened the "Spring Garden House," described by one traveler as "a cozy, home-like, well-built hotel." The United States Government meanwhile offered its sanction by authorizing a post office. Resultant publicity drew attention and additional settlers, some of whom chose to redirect a portion of local agricultural production from citrus to vegetable crops for Northern markets.[21]

Beautiful Spring Garden Springs, now DeLeon Springs State Park, drew tourists and settlers to the Spring Garden vicinity beginning in the 1870s. (Collection of the author.)

If Lawrence Brown knew anything from his Archer work experience by 1878, it was the care and propagation of vegetable crops for distant markets. Census records suggest that he first lent that expertise to an English "agriculturalist" named Benjamin B. Debbin, whose farming operation lay near that of G. H. Norris's main associate Charles Delano, also of Illinois. Brown's geographic proximity to Delano was to play a major role in his advancement at Spring Garden, although an unexpected and unlikely ally initially aided his quest for opportunity. That man was Uriah Mitchell Bennett. A Confederate veteran from Georgia, Bennett served at the time of Brown's Spring Garden arrival as the community's first postmaster. In key respects, he defied stereotypical expectations. A fervent Primitive Baptist minister as well as a far-sighted investor, Bennett took seriously his church's injunction to embrace all, regardless of race, within the fellowship of faith. Accordingly, he welcomed Brown warmly to the Spring Garden community.[22]

Uriah Mitchell Bennett. The Primitive Baptist minister and Confederate veteran served Spring Garden as postmaster upon L. B. Brown's arrival in 1878 and later encouraged the young man's real estate development activities at DeLeon Springs. (From Florida Agriculturalist, *January 17, 1906.)*

Lawrence, meanwhile, had begun to feel wary of his AME connections following the Alachua political debacle and in 1878 found himself drawn instead to Bennett's ministry. Thus, when the young man in September 1881 chose a life partner in 22-year-old Elizabeth "Bettie" Washington, he asked Bennett to perform the service. The pastor thereafter encouraged Brown's personal advancement by selling him, in early 1882, a five-acre parcel of land located just north of property that he intended to develop once railroads had begun the transformation of Spring Garden. As will be seen, by 1886, Bennett's tract had evolved into the town of DeLeon Springs, and Lawrence was poised to become a developer himself. Already, in May 1882, Brown had converted to the Baptist faith. Two years later he underwent ordination as a deacon. During that period of time, area Primitive Baptists boasted no organized church that they could attend closer to Spring Garden than at Pierson, located a dozen miles to the north. However, in early 1885 St. Johns Missionary Baptist Church opened its doors locally for black worshippers. Lawrence's devotion to the Missionary Baptist cause dated from that moment or soon afterward.[23]

On September 29, 1881, Rev. U. M. Bennett presided at the Spring Garden marriage of L. B. Brown and Elizabeth "Bettie" Washington. (From Marriage License Application Records, Volusia County Records Management Center, DeLand.) v

While U. M. Bennett's mentorship ushered Brown toward his Bartow future as developer and builder, his apprenticeship in those occupations rested in other hands. Reliable sources offer little detail regarding specific influences, but the most likely benefactor in that regard was G. H. Norris's friend Charles Delano. Ties between Brown and Delano materialized about 1881 when English planter Debbin departed Spring Garden. Coincidentally, Delano—a Democrat—had achieved election as Volusia's state senator, a position that he maintained through most of the decade. "While a resident of Ottawa," his Illinois hometown newspaper declared upon his initial nomination, "no citizen stood higher in the estimation of our people, who attested their appreciation of him by electing him to the honorable office of Mayor and other public positions, and it was only because he was always such a square, outspoken democrat that in this darkly republican region he failed to attain higher honors." Because his legislative responsibilities and other business interests compelled repeated absences, the new senator meanwhile required skilled and dependable assistance at Spring Garden in carrying on varied construction and developmental projects in which he was interested, contributions a capable man such as Brown could offer.[24]

One business initiative in particular dominated Delano's agenda and those of his allies. The senator well understood the necessity for early completion of a railroad to his community. That benchmark moment would bring the blessing of speedy transportation of crops to northern markets and of tourists and settlers to Volusia County. Perhaps, it also would open new outlets to the south in Cuba, the Caribbean, and South America. Described as "a practical railroad man of protracted and extensive experience," Delano emerged in short order as a leading force within state government for railroad construction and the granting of state lands in support of such endeavors. By March 4, 1881, he had achieved legislative passage and gubernatorial approval of a charter for the Palatka and Indian River Railway Company. The act authorized the company to construct a line from Putnam County down the St. Johns to Sanford and then eastwardly to the Atlantic. Among the founding directors who lived at Spring Garden were G. H. Norris; U. M. Bennett; and one-time ambassador to Singapore, personal friend of Abraham Lincoln, early Republican Party advocate, and future Volusia County Judge Isaac Stone. Henry DeLand, namesake of the town of DeLand, joined them.[25]

Delano's leadership of the Palatka and Indian River Railway by no means reached its end with the charter's approval. Appreciative directors immediately named him the line's first president. Financial and other challenges thereafter impeded Delano's ability to inaugurate construction on the line until 1884. When he was prepared to move ahead, he entrusted labor on the project to black workers recruited in good part in South Carolina and Maryland. More than a few of those individuals eventually decided to remain in the Spring Garden vicinity. They settled primarily at Glenwood, a village situated immediately below Spring Garden Center as the area's tiny business district was called. These men and their families formed the membership core for St. Johns Missionary Baptist Church and Mount Olive AME Church. Their presence in Glenwood could be attributed to Delano's construction there of "a palatial residence" that awed locals and visitors for years thereafter. Lawrence and Bettie lived close to Delano. The couple supplemented their income by operating their home as a boarding house.[26]

Through 1884 and into 1885, the steel rails inched toward Spring Garden, DeLand, and Sanford. By summer and fall 1885, sharp-minded businessmen were pressing plans tailored to take advantage of the changes about to rock their neighborhood. U. M. Bennett, for one, implemented his long-held scheme of town development, laying out before year's end what in 1886 became the Town of DeLeon Springs. As centerpiece, Bennett created the famed DeSoto Springs Hotel to lure tourists for hunting, fishing, and spring bathing. G. H. Norris's brother, A. Hart Norris, likewise endeavored to seize opportunity. Railroad plans called for the local depot to be located northeast of Spring Garden Springs (sometimes then called DeSoto Springs). In the circumstances, Norris offered the "new town of Spring Garden." It lay "one mile from the celebrated Spring Garden Mineral Spring." As Hart advertised in December 1886: "It is handsomely laid out in streets, parks and lots, surrounded by larger out-lying lots for gardening and fruit growing. . . . The town has already a post office with two daily mails, a commodious and well-kept hotel, a general store, a saw and planing mill, a blacksmith and wagon shop, a church and a school."[27]

Spring Garden's tiny business district centered in the 1880s on the Fish and Lee General Store. (Florida Photographic Collection, Florida State Archives, Tallahassee.)

The explosion in local construction projects brought lucrative employment for the building skills Brown had developed in his seven or eight years' residence at Spring Garden; but by late 1885, it also meant that he had begun dealing in property on his own account. A 50 x 160 foot residential lot that he deeded on December 5 to Frank W. Taylor, at a time when DeLeon Springs had not yet been named, represented the first of numerous sales. By February 1886—about the time the Jacksonville, Tampa, and Key West Railroad, as it was called then, had arrived—his deeds finally could define the lot's location by reference to "the map of DeSota Springs now known as DeLeon Spring." Lawrence's introduction to community development clearly came in the earliest days of the Spring Garden railroad boom.[28]

As chance would have it, relative prosperity arrived at just the right time for Brown. His father Peter, who had relocated to Deland about 1882 with Lawrence's mother Catherine, had passed away on June 14, 1885. Peter had died concerned for his beloved wife yet knowing that he could rely on Lawrence to protect her. The family Bible recorded, "Father Peter Brown's last request: I want you to take your mother with you as long as she lives, for I know you will take care of her." The entry added of Peter's last wishes: "Your Bro. Jos. owes me $40.00. I want you to get it, and give it all to your mother." Lawrence faithfully complied with his father's wishes. In that era before Social Security, such a responsibility carried with it a price tag. All surviving indications are that Brown happily shouldered the costs. Responsibility for Catherine's needs probably explained a family memory that Lawrence traveled the state during the 1880s as a Bible salesman. The Spring Garden area, for all of its growth by the mid-to-late 1880s, continued to reflect a seasonal orientation, with many property owners present principally during the winter months. In their absence, businesses of all kinds—including the building trades and land sales—lagged. As railroad construction during the period increasingly opened new areas of Florida for potential Bible sales, Lawrence, during summer months, easily could have taken time away from day-to-day responsibilities to explore the state as he bolstered family finances.[29]

Coincidentally, railroad transportation had reached Bartow in Polk County on January 8, 1885. One local resident called it "the grandest holiday ever known in Bartow." Just as at Archer and Spring Garden, black men had built the rails and more than a few had decided to make the place their home. Given that the area chronically lacked the availability of a reliable labor force, whites for the most part welcomed the new arrivals. Soon, individuals such as Jack C. Longworth had advanced in construction and other businesses. Institutions had begun to flourish. Among them Providence Baptist Church, today known as First Providence Missionary Baptist Church, traced its origins to the antebellum era while St. James AME now joined in serving the community. Soon, the population had grown sufficiently to compel the attention of a developer. A white man named William F. Britt opened a subdivision that he called Brittsville, strategically located within easy walking distance of the railroad depot in the northwestern part of town.[30]

By the decade's end, the AME Zion Church also had set its sights on Bartow and its thriving black community. "This is in South Florida, the new country that's just begun to be peopled up," one of its ministers proclaimed in early 1889. "Here our people can obtain good and valuable homes, with half the money it would take to go to California. They could come here and secure their home, and I believe, do equally as well, if not better. This country is rich and fertile. A few years ago one might travel for hundreds of miles and would see nothing but a vast forest, abounding with lakes, rivers, creeks, fish and game of all kinds with no facilities for traveling except for a few ox carts. But now, most every direction, you can hear the puff and whistle of the iron horse as he rushes past orange groves and through this vast depopulated forest, by means of which a great many villages and towns are being planted here and there throughout these regions. Let our people immigrate here and grow up with the country."[31]

At whatever moment Lawrence got around to visiting Bartow, he would have perceived excellent opportunity; yet, for the time being he remained happily a Spring Garden resident. Even politics seemed to be shifting in his favor there. Republicans for the first time seized a Volusia County state legislative seat in 1886 and followed up on that landmark event two years later with other victories that included Isaac Stone's election as county judge. By 1889, though, signs pointed to the virtual elimination of blacks and Republicans from politics in most areas of Florida. Early that year Democrats in the state legislature enacted several laws aimed at consolidating power for their party. Most importantly, they approved a poll tax. That measure imposed a cash fee for registering to vote and required registration as a prerequisite for voting. Within two years, voting participation plummeted among poor whites as well as among blacks. In 1888, Republicans could offer to state voters—with some expectation of competitive races—a bi-racial ticket, one that included Isaac Stone as candidate for superintendent of public instruction. No possibility existed thereafter for competition in statewide contests until well after the poll tax's repeal half a century later.[32]

As the years passed, additional setbacks added to the complications of life at Spring Garden. Tragically for Lawrence, his wife Elizabeth Washington Brown apparently succumbed during the late 1880s, possibly in childbirth. Notably also, in December 1887, community founder George H. Norris passed away. "Though holding no public position," a friend wrote, "he was a man of great prominence from his phenomenal energy, keen business tact, and public spirit, and was held in high esteem." With the loss of Norris, the energy and spirit required to advance Spring Garden ebbed. The trend continued on October 9, 1890, with the Glenwood death of

Isaac Stone. Charles Delano by early 1889 had departed the state senate. He attempted to revive area vitality but endured his own family ordeal in September 1890 with the loss of his wife Hannah. As late as summer 1892, though, Delano persisted in pressing his dreams, ones that included construction of a railroad down the Atlantic coast to Key West. Unfortunately, those dreams had to be realized by another man, Henry Flagler, after Delano died at Glenwood in November 1893.[33]

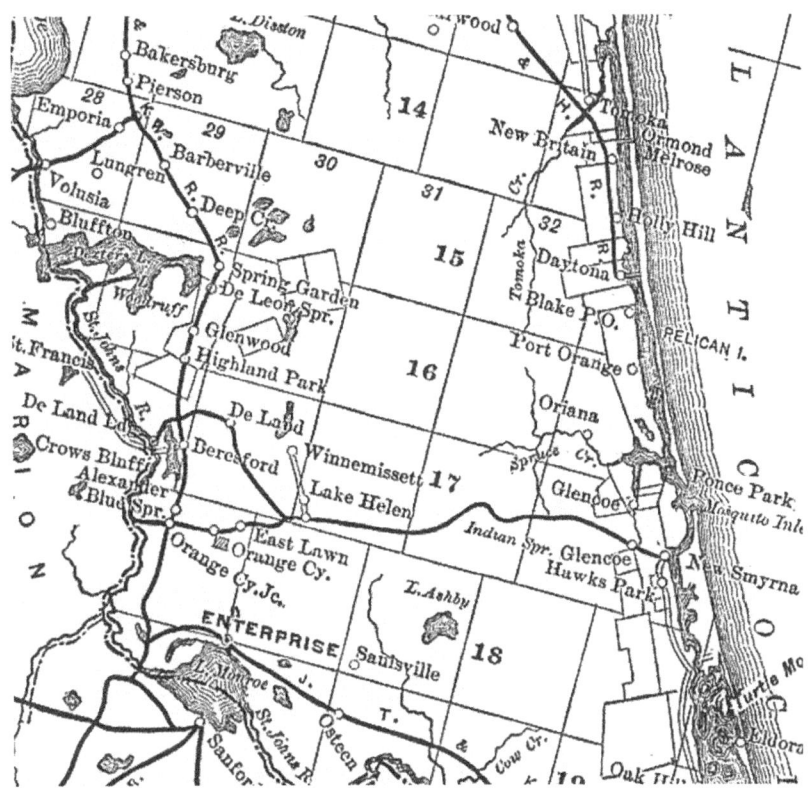

An 1890 view of Volusia County, Florida, illustrating the passage of the Jacksonville, Tampa and Key West Railroad through Spring Garden, DeLeon Springs, and Glenwood. (From Charles Ledyard Norton, A Handbook of Florida.*)*

As economic conditions and prospects dipped for Lawrence at Spring Garden in the late 1880s and early 1890s, he began to consider relocating toward brighter possibilities. Available evidence suggests that, at some point between G. H. Norris's death in late 1887 and Charles Delano's demise six years later, Brown began to spend at least part of each year—summers, most likely—at Bartow. Most probably, the pivotal moment came in early 1889 when the town excitedly greeted the arrival of a veritable gold rush after discovery nearby of massive deposits of phosphates. "Gone Wild on Phosphates," one headline screamed. Another declared, "Polk County in the Throes of the Craze for Sudden Wealth." Property values at Bartow raced to new heights, while settlers anxious to share in the wealth poured into town. Few businessmen, especially ones born a slave on Florida's remote frontier during an Indian War, were better prepared to take advantage than was Lawrence B. Brown. In doing so, he helped to transform a community. Meanwhile, he created a legacy that continues to merit our respect today.[34]

Chapter 2

Lawrence Brown's Life in Bartow

Lawrence B. Brown's Early Days in Bartow

Lawrence Bernard Brown arrived in the booming town of Bartow, Florida in the late 1880s hoping to make a life for himself as an entrepreneur.

Along with the discovery of phosphate deposits, the arrival of the railroad in the mid-1880s brought a rapid increase in Bartow's population. Reliable transportation enabled farmers to send their produce to other markets and opened up this frontier to other parts of the country. Lawrence Brown, already familiar with the importance of the railroad in bringing economic prosperity to an area, was most likely influenced to settle in Bartow by the railroad's presence. Bartow's population more than tripled from around 400 in 1885 to 1,386 by 1890. By 1895 it was the thirteenth largest town in Florida.[1] Large-scale mining of phosphate propelled the growth and gave Bartow the nickname "Queen City" of Polk County.[2]

Downtown Bartow Circa 1885 Photo courtesy Florida State Archives/Library of Florida

The good times, unfortunately, were not to last. The census of 1900 found Bartow fared poorly with only fifty-two new residents over the decade. From 1900 to 1905, the town lost seventy-eight persons and found itself left with a population of only 1,905.[3]

Social Conditions After the Civil War

Shortly after the Civil War ended slavery in 1865, the country began to move toward bringing black males fully into society with the same privileges as white men. The 1866 Civil Rights Act granted citizenship to black males with the same rights as those possessed by white citizens. Ratification of the 14th Amendment to the U.S. Constitution gave rights granted by the Bill of Rights to the formerly enslaved two years later. Then, ratification of the 15th Amendment in 1870 granted African American men the right to vote.

These positive actions eventually faced stiff opposition from Jim Crow laws. These laws had their roots in the 1865 Black Codes, mentioned in chapter one. Jim Crow laws, first enacted in Tennessee in 1871, were meant to marginalize former enslaved persons by denying them rights and opportunities. Other southern states adopted similar laws over the decades that followed, ultimately making it unlawful for black persons to use public accommodations that had been set aside or reserved solely for whites. This led to racially segregated schools throughout the South. Additionally, in 1889 Florida passed the first poll tax which prohibited most black men from voting as they could not afford to register. This also kept many low-income white men from voting.

Importantly, the Supreme Court in 1896 approved the "separate but equal" doctrine which, in practice, soon evolved into the separate and unequal doctrine.[4] Life became even more dangerous for African American citizens.

Brown Begins His Bartow Endeavor

In spite of these efforts to make black citizens second-class members of society, Lawrence Brown had experienced success in his young life and moved to Bartow fully expecting to become a successful businessman. He had money in his pocket from his previous work in Volusia County and felt confident in his abilities. Yet, for a black man born into slavery this was no easy dream as political and societal forces worked against black men with such high hopes.

Most of the laborers who worked in Bartow's growing businesses and industries during the era were black men. Because of labor shortages, they earned good wages. Accordingly, they also required decent housing. Lawrence Brown possessed just the right experience to fill their need.

In years immediately prior to or after 1890, Brown applied his skills and talents to the task. He began with the purchase of two acres of land from Louis N. Milam for $300. The tract lay in "East Bartow" near the railroad tracks. On the property he erected houses for rent and sale. He called his development "Brown's Estate" and later changed it to "Brown's Subdivision."[5]

During April and May 1892, Brown purchased from Milam two additional acres of land for $155. On this tract—located on Second Avenue (now L. B. Brown Avenue)—he built his two-story family home. The site stood out for its close proximity to Main Street and because of its proximity to a railroad passenger station.[6]

Lawrence carried out his dying father's last request to care for his mother. He lived in the home with his mother, Catherine Brown, until her death in 1923. The house included a workshop located on its north side that served as his office where he repaired furniture, silvered mirrors, made and repaired umbrellas, and sold Bibles. The first deed for this property was held in his mother's name. Black men often resorted to this tactic so as not to appear pretentious in these perilous times. However, it is possible that Catherine purchased the land with her own resources.

Hallie Mae

Despite the difficult social conditions, Brown's activities expanded. At times he was a speculator, developer, builder, real estate broker, banker, self-taught lawyer, carpenter, furniture maker, glass silversmith, salesman, well digger, and engineer.[7] During the mid-1890s Brown travelled to his native town of Archer and to nearby Micanopy. While there he spent time with a young woman, Arjancy Bassett. This relationship resulted in the birth of his daughter Hallie Mae on December 10, 1894. No formal marriage ensued. Brown recognized his responsibilities, though, and supported her until his death in 1941. They routinely kept in touch through letters and occasional visits.

Hallie Mae was raised by her mother and step-father. She married Horace Goodwin in 1912. Their four children were Marcellus, Fredonia, Arabella, and Louvenia. Hallie usually took youngest daughter Lovenia on trips to see her father. They spent a good deal of the time in the workshop or else on the front porch where Annie Belle, Brown's third wife, would serve them refreshing drinks.

Hallie Mae actively served her church as organist, pianist, and in other roles. She made her living as a master beautician and stood out as a charter member of the Orange Blossom Cosmetology State Association. Hallie Mae Godwin, Brown's oldest child, died March 30, 1977.

About two years after building his own home, Brown subdivided the remainder of his property into lots to build homes to rent or sell. There were eight lots, each approximately 70 feet wide and 156 feet in depth. His subdivision lay at the northwestern edge of East Bartow, which became one of Bartow's largest ethnic neighborhoods.[8]

Meanwhile, as man of intelligence and deeply held values, Lawrence Brown extended his reach into the community. Significantly, he was among the founding members of the Mt.

Gilboa Missionary Baptist Church in East Bartow where he served as the first clerk. Very active in church work throughout his life, he contributed generously to the needs of the poor.[9] Brown also encouraged the congregation of his church with his generosity by contributing about one-fourth of his rental income to the church.

A decade or so after reaching Bartow, he married for the second time on September 8, 1897, at 7:30 p.m. His bride, Laura Lee, was the daughter of one of his tenants, Henry Lee. Sadly, their expected child was still-born. The marriage suffered from this and other factors. Brown heard from others that in his absence, Laura Lee treated his mother poorly. According to surviving accounts, she personally directed harsh words at his mother and refused to fix her meals. When Lawrence returned home early one day, he observed Laura's behavior. He moved to dissolve their marriage.[10] They parted on October 12, 1897. Happy to end the union, he noted in his Bible that the marriage lasted "One month, five days, and three hours. To the minute."

The Brown Journals

Beyond notations in his Bible, and fortunately for those who came afterward, Brown left copious writings. An organized man, he kept records of his business transactions as well as other events important to him in detailed journals. These journals and other writings allow insightful glimpses of his life and times.

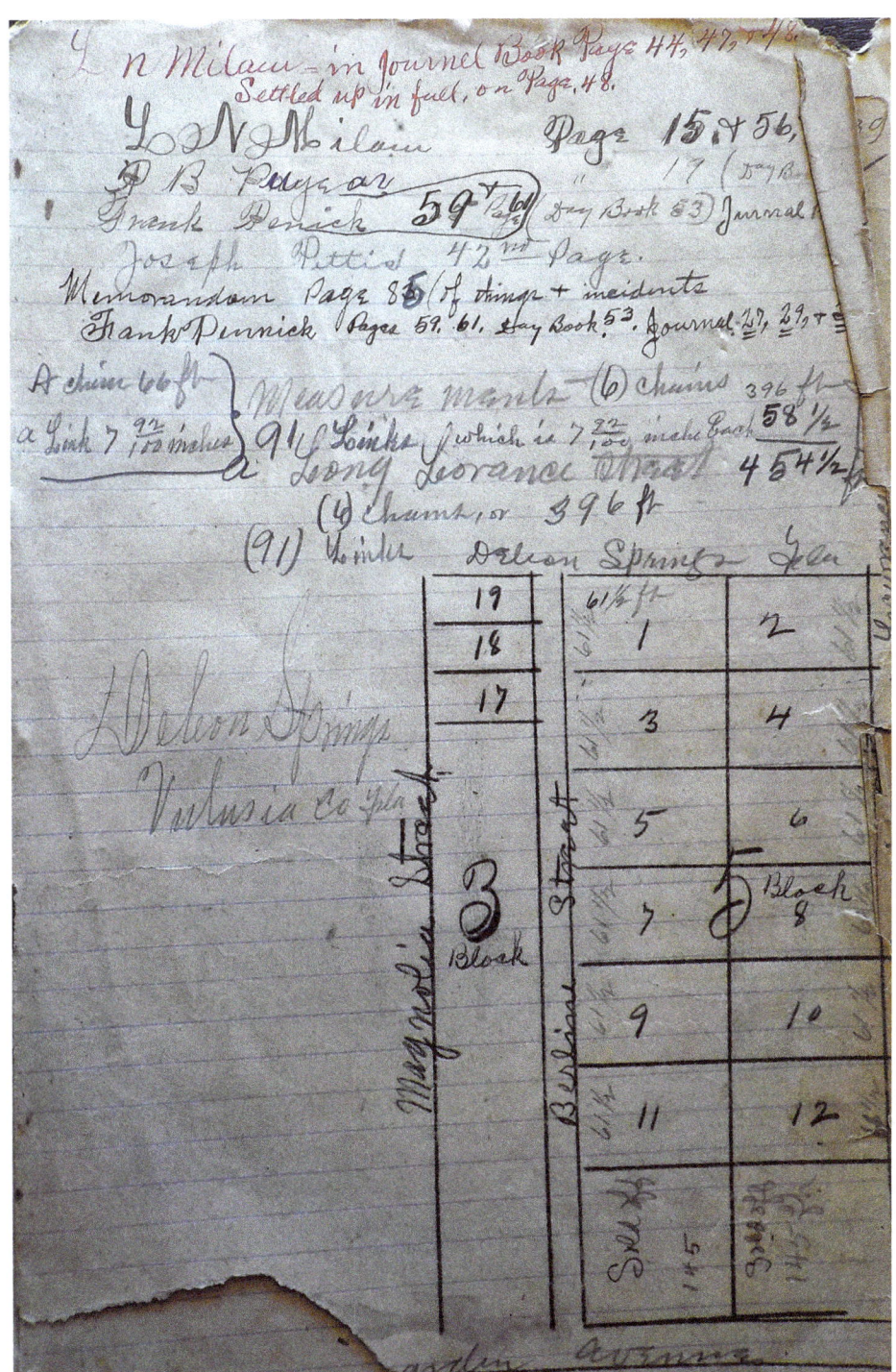

This ledger page illustrates a parcel of land that Brown developed in DeLeon Springs in Volusia County. L. N. Milan, whose name is prominently written at the top of the ledger, sold Brown much of the land he later purchased in Bartow. This loose page likely came from one of his much earlier journals as it is not as neat and well organized as those dated from 1895 and the years following.

FROM SLAVERY TO COMMUNITY BUILDER

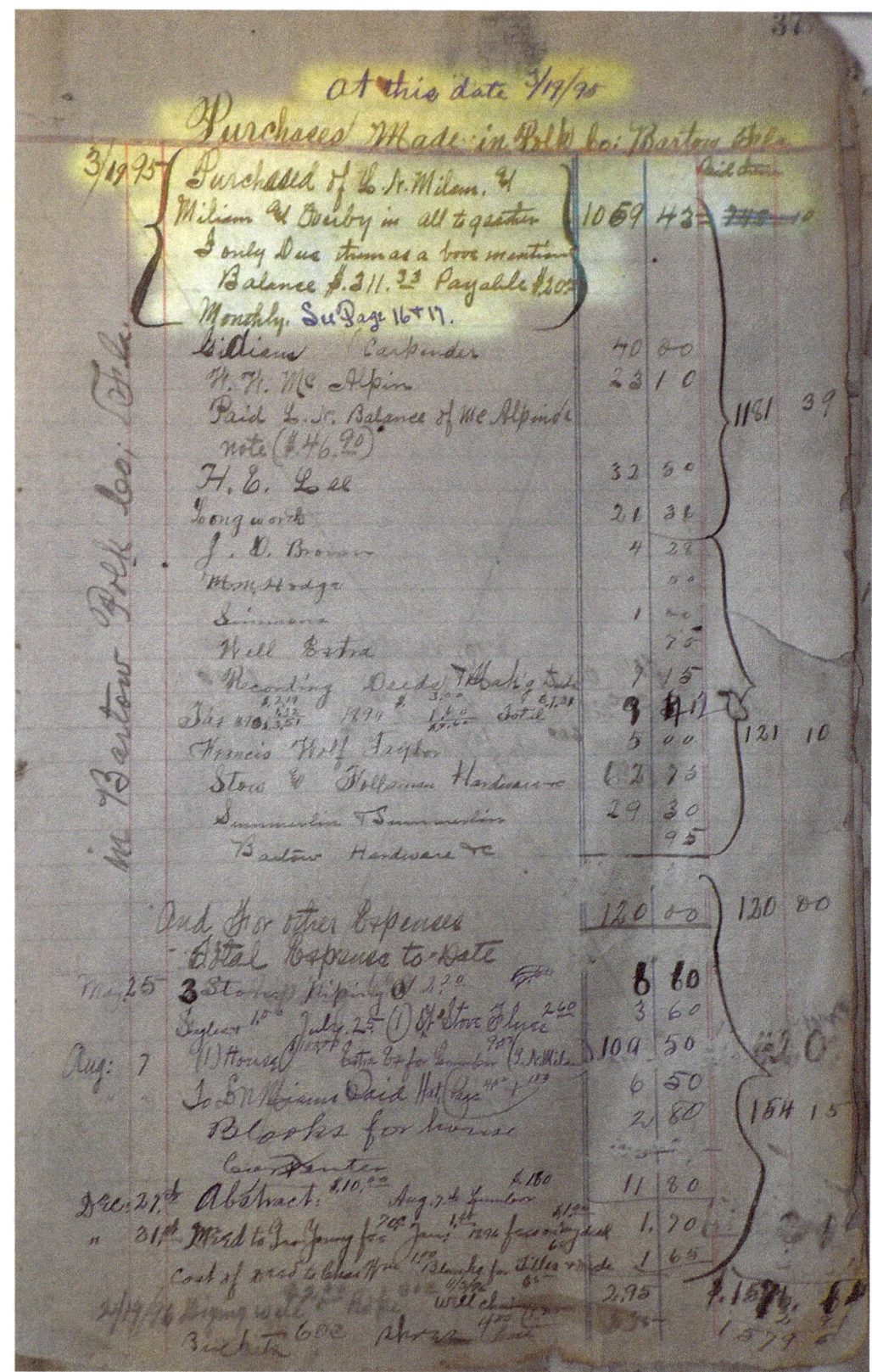

This page is dated March 19, 1895. At this time, Lawrence Brown is in Bartow. Notice how organized this entry is compared to the one shown on the previous page.

The top portion of this page reads as follows:

At this date 3/19/95
Purchases made in Polk County: Bartow, Fla
3/19/95 Purchased of L. N. Milam and Miliam and Overby in all together $1009.43
only Due items as above mentioned
Balance $311.33 Payable $20.00
Monthly. See Page 16+17.

The large dollar amount of the transaction indicates that it probably involved the purchase of land. The remainder of the page lists other purchases he had made and expenses paid in Bartow such as the recording of deeds and buying material to build houses. Obviously, he had become thoroughly familiar with legal requirements as well as construction skills.

In all, Brown erected over fifty houses in the Bartow area. He designed the structures, ordered the materials, hired work crews, and kept the financial records—doing the various jobs that several persons with different skills would accomplish in a modern-day construction organization.

These journals reflect something remarkable. Brown had been born into slavery, possessed little education, and lived in an environment within which black people—especially successful black persons—often faced disrespect and even scorn from many in white society. Still, his outstanding personal qualities allowed him to overcome obstacles and succeed. He managed to work with white town officials and white merchants as well as with work crews consisting mostly of black men.

Brown's Rental Contract with Ben Knight

Tough in business, he nonetheless remained a compassionate man. This next series of ledger pages affords insight into Lawrence Brown, the person. They provide us specifically with the story of how Brown accommodated Ben Knight, a worker who experienced difficulty keeping up with payments arising out of their agreement.

FROM SLAVERY TO COMMUNITY BUILDER

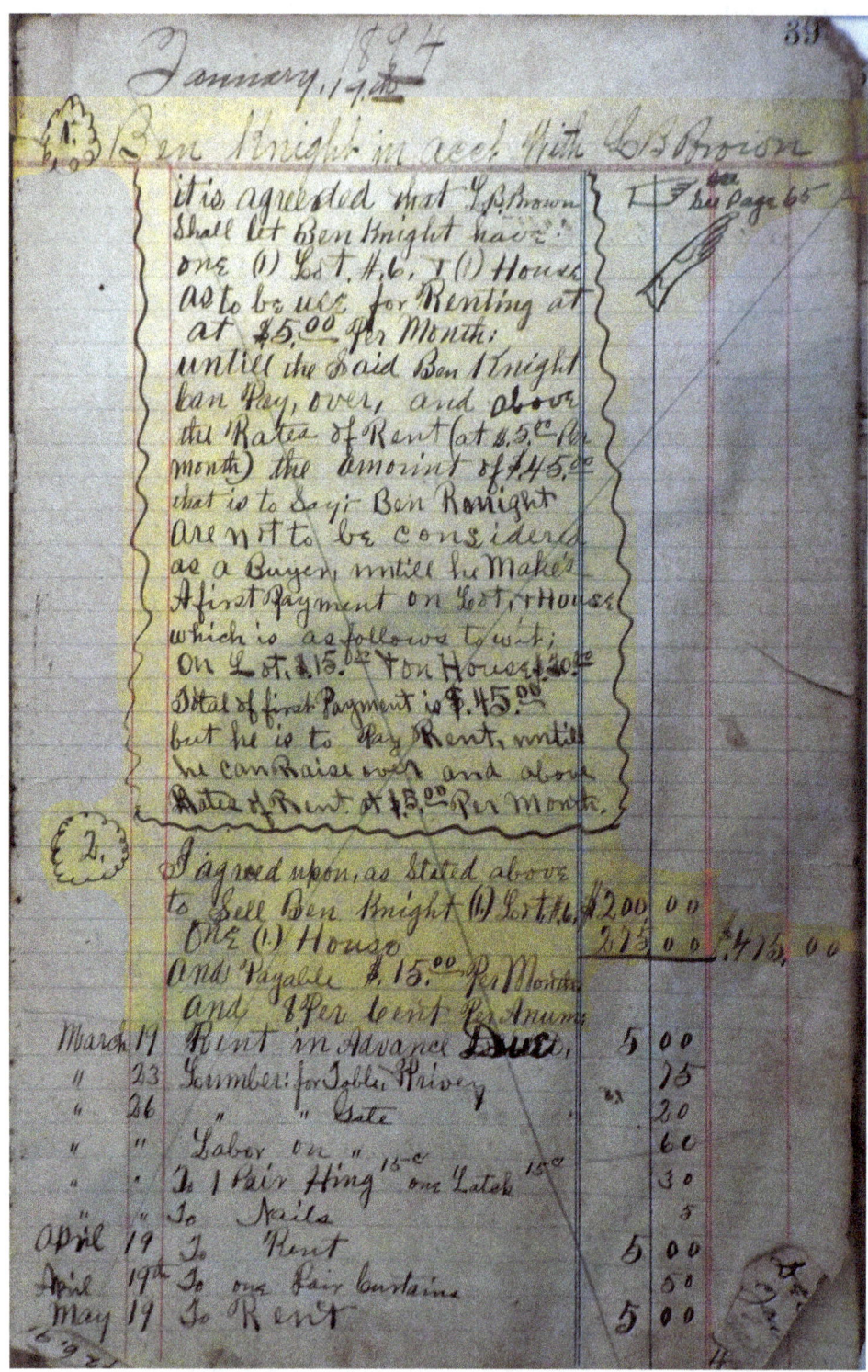

The saga commenced under the date January 19, 1894, when Lawrence Brown recorded the agreement. Rent-to-own is a commonplace approach in our day; Lawrence may have stood out, however, as one of the first to have a rent-to-own contract with a renter in Bartow.

January 19th 1894

1. Ben Knight in account with LB Brown
It is agreed that L.B. Brown shall let Ben Knight have
one (1) lot #6 and (1) house
as to be used for renting at
$5.00 per month:
until the said Ben Knight
can pay over and above
the rate of rent (at $5.00 per
month) the amount of $45.00.
That is to say, Ben Knight
are not to be considered
as a buyer until he makes
a first payment on lot and house
which is as follows to wit:
On lot $15.00 and on house $30.00.
Total of first payment is $45.00.
But he is to pay rent until
he can raise over and above
rate of rent at $5.00 per month.

2. I agreed upon, as stated above,
to sell Ben Knight (1) lot #6 $200.00
One (1) House $275.00
And payable $15.00 per month and 8 per cent interest per annum

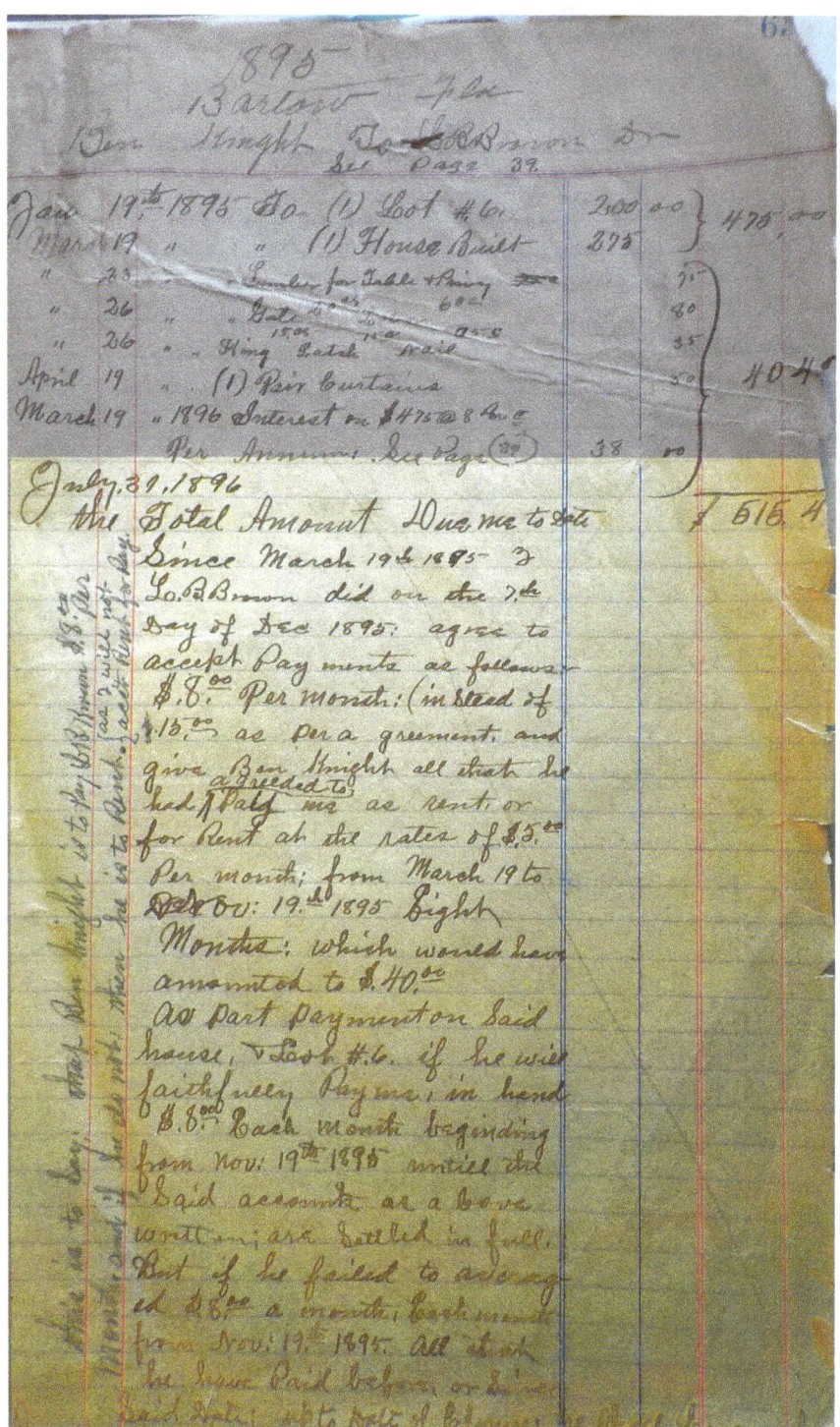

This next page lists some of Lawrence Brown's expenses that he added to Ben's account and the interest for the year. In the agreement he lowers Ben's payment from $15.00 per month to $8.00. Lawrence displayed benevolence by helping him to buy the house and lot by means of applying the rent payments to the cost of the house.

The writing on the left side of the ledger declares: This is to say that Ben Knight is to pay LB Brown $8.00 per month and if he is not then he is to rent {as I will not accept rent for pay.

July 31, 1896

The total amount due me to date Since March 19th 1895 I LB Brown did on the 7th day of Dec. 1895: agree to accept payments as follows $8.00 per month (instead of $15.00 as per agreement. And give Ben Knight all that he had agreed to pay me as rent, or for rent at the rates of 5.00 per month; from March 19 to Nov. 19th 1895 eight months: which would have amounted to $40.00 as part payment on said house + lot #6 if he will faithfully pay me in hand $8.oo each month beginning from Nov. 19th 1895 until the said accounts as above written are settled in full. But if he failed to average $8.00 a month. Each month from Nov. 19th 1895. All that he have paid before or since said date up to date of closure he shall lose from rent of said house.

This next page shows that Ben did indeed struggle to make payments. Lawrence adjusted the agreement one more time.

L B Brown do agree to sell lot #6 + house to Ben Knight for the above amount as agreement if he will pay $8.00 per month. If he fail to pay or average $8.00 per month I will rent him the house at $3.00 per month.

L. B. Brown adjusted the agreement allowing Ben to pay just $3.00 per month rent if unable to make the $8.00 per month payments to buy the house and lot.

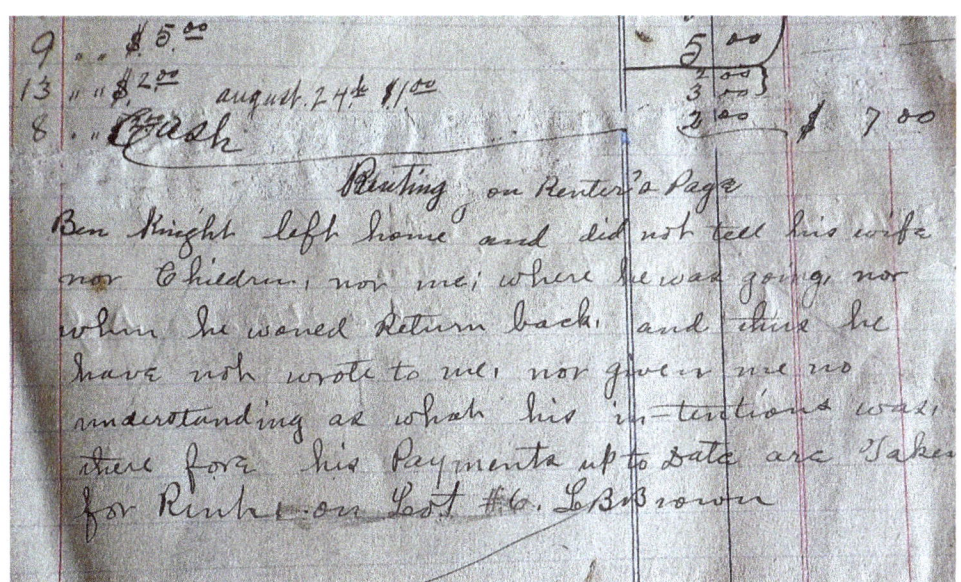

The unfortunate result

Ben Knight left home and did not tell his wife nor children nor me where he was going nor when he would return back and thus he have not wrote to me, nor given me no understanding what his intentions was therefore his payments up to date are taken for rent on lot #6.   L B Brown

Brown was left to wonder what had happened to Ben Knight. Polk County had passed through several rough years. The Panic of 1893, a national economic depression, had hurt the phosphate industry and people had lost jobs. Then, in September 1894 a hurricane caused flooding and seriously damaged agriculture. The Freeze of 1895 destroyed much of the citrus industry and other agriculture. More jobs were lost.[11]

Seen within this context, Lawrence's adjustment of Ben's mortgage agreement might have reflected his way of helping someone going through a difficult time that had arisen due to forces beyond his control. Another possibility is that Ben may have been killed and his body never discovered. Up to the time that he disappeared, Ben seems to have been trying to establish himself locally. Thereafter, he fails to appear on any local census.

Payments to Milam and Overby

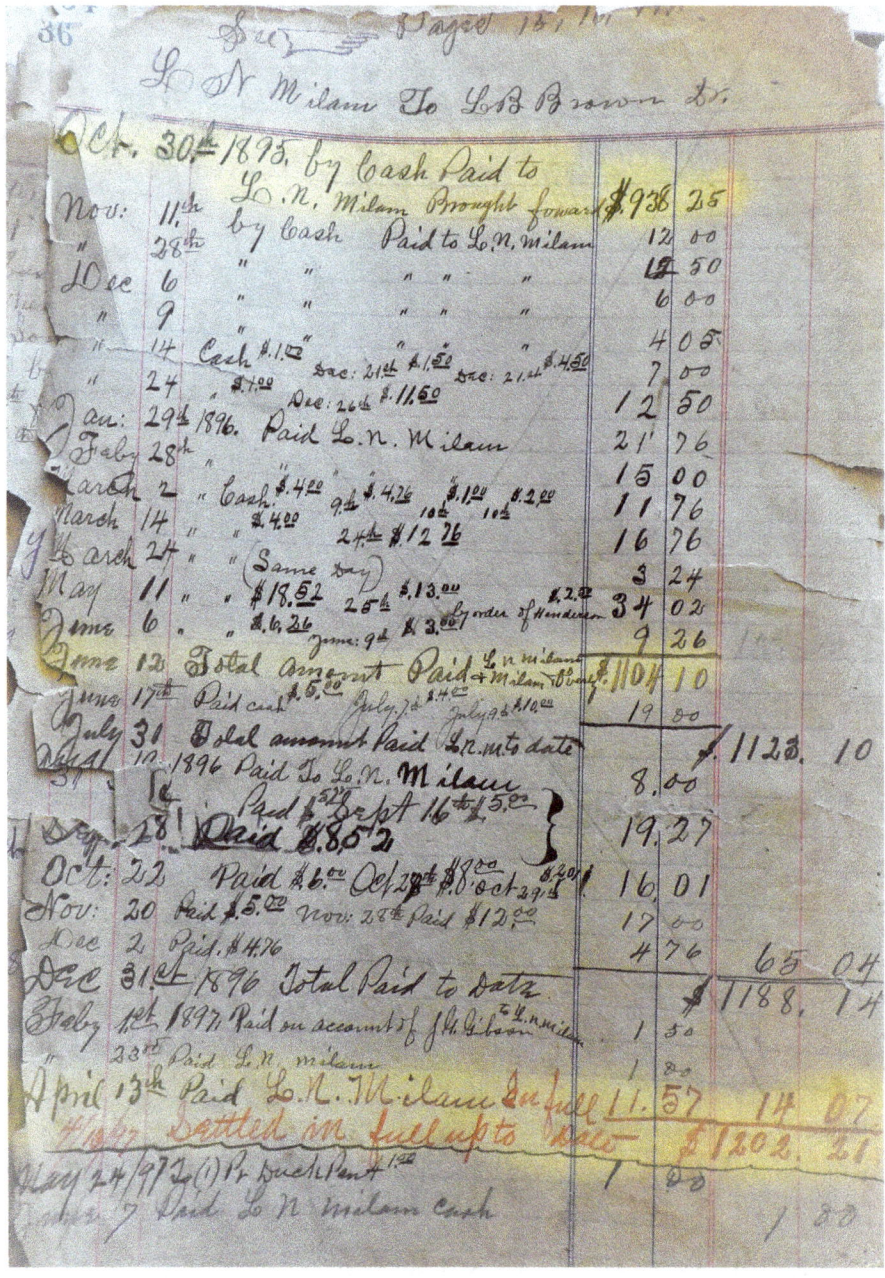

The above page shows continuing payments to Milam and Overby.

Oct. 30th 1895 by cash paid to
L. N. Milam brought forward $938.25

An entry of June 12th:

June 12 Total amount paid
L. N. Milam + Milam + Overby $1104.10

Finally, near the bottom, written in red ink to emphasize its importance:

4/12/97 Settled in full up to date $1202.20

Haircut Agreement

Brown remained, despite losses such as those involved with Ben Knight, an astute businessman with an eye kept carefully on the bottom line. He even contracted for haircuts by the year, as described here. Other entries further underscore his frugality and the care that he took with his money.

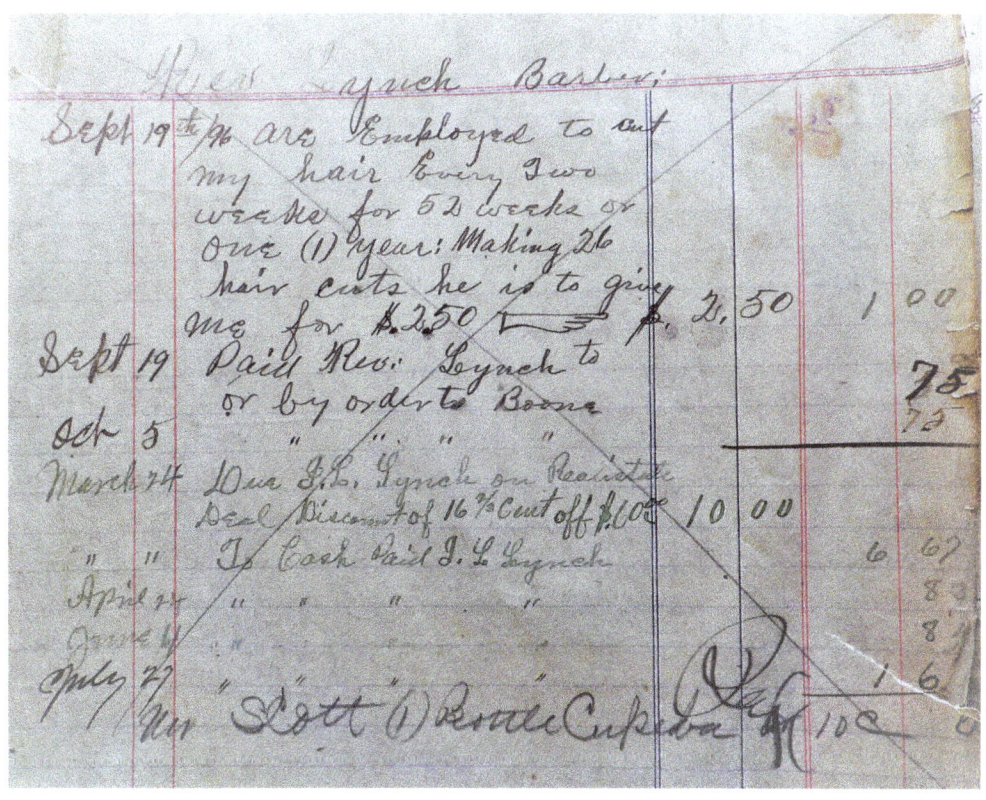

This 1896 agreement was for one haircut every two weeks for one year for the sum of $2.50.

Renters Payments

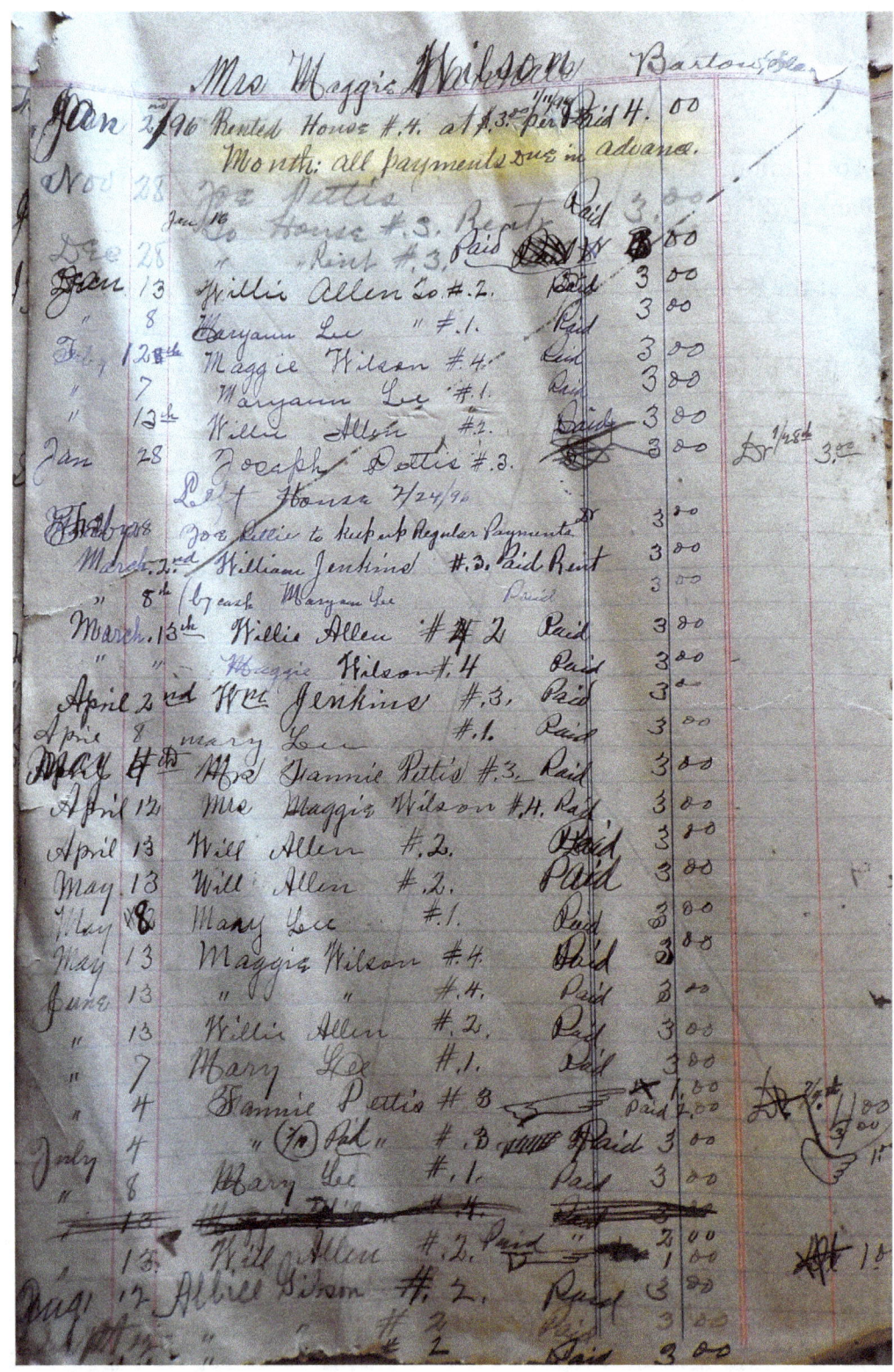

This ledger page records payments made by his renters. All payments due in advance.

Schooling and the Community

As previously mentioned, the late 1890s brought economic hardships for Bartowans and, especially, those employed in the town's core industries. As Lawrence Brown's rental income depended upon such workers, he necessarily endured consequences of the economic slowdown.

Thanks to prevailing wage rates, a prosperous black community had emerged in the area of Bartow during the late 1880s and early 1890s. The Summerlin Institute, although a symbol of Bartow's emergence into the modern era, served only white students. However, successful African-American residents such as Andy Moore, Prince Johnson, Jack Longworth, and Ned Green pressed for better educational opportunities and civic programs for black children and adults. Religious institutions such as First Providence Missionary Baptist, St. James African Methodist Episcopal (AME), and also the African Methodist Episcopal Zion Church (AMEZ), which took pains to focus on Bartow in its ministry and educational efforts, helped to enhance the black communities.[12]

Early on, this leadership led to educational innovation. First Providence Missionary Baptist Church held classes for black children until around 1887 when, according to Bartow city commission minutes, the city appropriated $5000 to aid Summerlin Institute and "five hundred dollars to construct a school for the Colored children of Bartow." This appropriation allowed the erection of a two-story building on what is now Polk Street. The facility's first floor held classrooms; a large open auditorium filled the second. Theatrical performances and, eventually, movies also utilized the second floor to entertain residents.

The school benefitted tremendously from the caliber of its teachers. East Bartow resident Clarence C. Johnson, who stood out as a prominent member of the African-American community in the time of Lawrence Brown, is believed to have been the first certified black teacher in Polk County. Possessed of a solid educational background, Johnson often stood out as the first teacher assigned to a newly established black school. So accomplished was Johnson that he later rose to supervision of testing and certifying other black teachers. The bottom line—he was dedicated to teaching.

Pursuant to law, the school board appointed "well-connected" black and white men to serve as school supervisors. They reported directly to the school superintendent. Bartow's early black school supervisors included friends and associates of L.B. Brown such as Charles Henry Macon, Clarence C. Johnson, Ned Green, and Fred Waldon.[13]

Their job was not an easy one. The African-American community continually struggled to keep an educational program in Bartow for black children. On December 7, 1895—when the county school board ran short of money due to the Great Freeze—its members suspended the teacher of the Brittsville (West Bartow) school. The action closed the school indefinitely. The year 1896 saw the only other school for African American children in Bartow closed as well.

With the closings, black leaders and citizens rallied as the AME, AMEZ, and Baptist Churches banded together to support the availability of good educational opportunities for their children. The churches held a rally on March 28, 1897, to support this effort. AMEZ Bishop T. H. Lomax, a black man, donated land.

Finally, on May 4, 1897, the school board agreed to reimburse the building of the school: "On motion $225 was appropriated to the Colored school building in Bartow. The same to be paid when the building is finished and received by this board." It is noteworthy to the struggle of the black population to educate their children that they had to provide the land and pay for the construction while schools for white children were paid for with tax funds from black citizens as well as white citizens.

Thanks to the efforts of the churches and many individual residents, construction of a new school ensued.[14] In early 1897, contractor L. N. Milam began his work and, on September 7, the school board accepted the building.

An elaborate two-day event scheduled for August 19 and 20 was planned for laying the cornerstone. The event attracted statewide attention. Railroads offered discount tickets for those traveling from other towns in Florida. The event included baseball games between various Polk County towns, a service at the St. James AME Church followed by a procession to the school site, a welcome by the mayor, speeches, competitions for monetary prizes, and entertainment. Money raised by this event went to the school.

The new facility carried the name Union Academy. Notably, it eventually became Polk County's first high school for black students in 1928. On June 4, Union Academy reached a historic milestone by awarding to Lela Burkett the first high school diploma to a black person in Polk County. A decade later, the editor of the Bartow newspaper would call the school "one of the best in Florida."

The first Union Academy building (1897) was located on Fifth Avenue, only three blocks from the Brown family home. All of Brown's seven children attended that school. His oldest daughter, Louvenia, served on the faculty as a teacher.

The successful struggle to build a school is impressive considering the racism black citizens had to deal with on a daily basis. On August 25, the *Courier-Informant* reported, "The building is a large substantial one, and our colored friends deserve much credit for their successful efforts in this work." However, just a few years later, July 26, 1899, an editorial stated "—It seems that educating the negroes simply makes them shiftless, idle, gambling, lustful devils good for nothing but the broadening of the chasm between the two races—."

Changes in Bartow from Early 1890s to Early 1900s

In the 1890s and early 1900s, as Lawrence Brown endeavored with the product of his labor to enhance his community, he and other Bartowans witnessed many additional improvements.

- In the early 1890s, clay of "a superior quality," discovered in the Bartow vicinity resulted in wooden sidewalks being replaced with clay. The town ordered property owners to pave them over with cement or brick. This clay was called "Bartow macadam."
- The clay played a prominent role in developing Polk County's system of roads. The city purchased fifteen mules, carts, and a street roller to begin paving the streets. An ordinance required all men between eighteen and forty-five (save for ministers, fire department members, and city officials) to work six days per year on the streets or—in lieu of working—pay $6.00. Local businessmen complained loudly to the city council.
- The smooth streets allowed bicycling to emerge as a favorite method of locomotion.
- The city employed a scavenger (garbage collector) and furnished buckets, a mule, and a cart.
- The installation of fifty oil street lamps in 1891 along Main Street as far as the South Florida Railroad Depot provided unprecedented light. The Lamp Lighter received thirty-five dollars per month.
- An 1892 report asserted that Bartow had become the phosphate city of the state. "To the great phosphate industry is due its phenomenal prosperity: in a radius of twelve miles around this city there are eight large phosphate plants in operation, each plant working not less than twenty-five men, and some as many as fifty."
- In midsummer 1893, Bartow claimed 2,500 people and two railroads.
- In 1894, the town purchased one thousand water oaks at twenty-five cents each and planted them along parkways.
- Construction also began on a water-works system and was completed the following year.
- The city organized a volunteer fire department consisting of two hose companies and a hook and ladder company.
- Electric lights finally became a reality on April 18, 1897.[15]

(Polk County Historical Quarterly) Bartow's Main Street, c. 1896.

1902 and 1904 proved banner years for Bartow. Residents approved a bond issue for street paving and installing a sewage system. Already, on January 21, 1902, Mayor W. H. Johnson had called up his Tampa counterpart and exchanged messages of good-will on behalf of the two cities, thus inaugurating long distance telephone service. The Peninsular Telephone Company's exchange formally opened February 11, 1902—an occasion of much rejoicing. Mrs. Ella Clark became the first, and only, operator. The city granted a franchise for a telephone system in 1904 for thirty years. In February of this same year, the residents viewed their first moving picture show, a one-night affair. However, some of the "illustrations" sparked controversy, clearly failing to please at least some local people.

Race Relations

In spite of racist Jim Crow laws, cordial relations continued to exist for some across the color line. A number of white citizens attended St. James AME Church when it laid a cornerstone for a new sanctuary on February 1, 1895. The same week, white persons participated in the Star of Zion AMEZ Church South Florida Conference in West Bartow.[16]

In spite of progress made, serious challenges remained. Bartow fared better than did many towns, thanks to its diverse economy. Unfortunately, 1895's Great Freeze harmed race relations significantly, bringing out racial divisions not apparent in better times. As the economy remained stagnant, jobs became scarce. Resulting competition between black workers and white workers prompted some white persons to consider African Americans as their enemies.[17]

Violence inflicted upon the race emerged as a serious problem. "As white persons pushed Jim Crow policies through the 1890s and early 1900s, enhanced tensions across the color line resulted in racial violence on a large scale," historian Canter Brown observed. Lynchings punctuated the passing months and years, with Florida in the lead on a per capita basis. Polk County for the most part—with the possible exception of the Mulberry vicinity—had resisted this trend from the early 1870s until 1901."[18] The pattern of mob violence as a means of racial social control, once begun, continued for decades.

The first in a series of tragic lynchings occurred in 1901, ending the increasingly uneasy truce between the two races. On May 28, a group of white citizens accused Fred Rochelle of raping a young white woman named Rena Taggert and then killing her. Rochelle fled. The black community anticipated reprisals. Anger built with the passage of time. The next day, two black men apprehended Rochelle and turned him over to Sheriff Dallas Tillis. A crowd of white men "took charge" of the prisoner at the jail and lynched him, burning him alive. Newspapers across the nation blared the horrible news. Some white residents, it must be noted, regretted the incident. Community leaders soon invited African-American church officials to visit Bartow to judge the white community for themselves. The meetings proved cordial and reports declared them a success.[19]

The Rochelle lynching took place in East Bartow, not too distant from Lawrence Brown's home. To have a mob torture and murder someone close to your neighborhood surely traumatized Brown, his mother, and their neighbors. In fact, such public executions were intended to instill fear in the black community.

In December 1903, a group of white men again acted to lynch a black man. Circumstantial evidence suggested that he attempted to murder the white general manager of a phosphate company. The sheriff foiled the mob's plan by taking the accused to Tampa for his safety. Later tried and convicted, the accused reportedly received a twenty-year prison sentence.

Then, in July 1906, a mob of white men killed two black men. A group of some fifty individuals intercepted the sheriff while escorting his prisoners to the county jail. The men shot the detainees to death. The mob suspected the men of murdering Ed Gardner, manager of the turpentine still for which they worked.[20]

Brown's Last Marriage

*Annie Belle Brown
May 24, 1880—
September 15, 1938*

During these turbulent times, Lawrence's third and last marriage took place. On July 13, 1909, at 5:30 pm, he wed Annie Bell Burnette. He had attained 53 years of age. Annie was 29. The age difference meant little at the time. Annie Bell's parents George and Lenora Granger had moved to Bartow from Georgia around 1900. Annie, a Georgia native living in Bartow, had been married to the now-deceased Benjamin Burnette, who owned a store where Lawrence did business. Burnette died in 1906.

The union proved a successful one. Lawrence and Annie raised seven children: Benjamin Burnette, (from Annie's first marriage,) Lavonia, Lorenzo, Clifford, Mary, Annie Belle, and Robert. Annie Bell, a devoted mother and conscientious housewife, brought considerable assets into the marriage. Given a flair for elegance, she made an ideal partner for Lawrence. Lawrence and Annie Belle's union lasted until her death in 1938.

Given his caring nature, Lawrence Brown became a loving father to his three-year-old stepson, treating Benjamin as though he were his own. An explosion and fire in the old Polk County courthouse tragically killed Benjamin while at work on February 12, 1942. He is buried in the Brown family plot in Bartow.

The *Polk County Record* reported on page one of their February 17, 1942, edition: "County Officials and courthouse employees contributed a sufficient amount of money Saturday to insure two payments on the home of the late Ben Burnett, Negro janitor, as a token of appreciation and a gesture of assistance to his family."

Annie Belle sadly endured serious health issues that at times required hospitalization. Lawrence's ledger records that he took his wife to the Clara Frye Hospital in Tampa for treatment. Frye, an African American nurse, established and operated the well-known hospital in the early 1910s. She founded the facility because other hospitals would not accept black patients. Frye accepted persons of all ethnicities. Robert, Annie's youngest child, reported that, as his mother's health worsened, his father spent large sums of money on her treatment to ensure that she received the best care. She often remained in the hospital for extended stays or else lived with a relative in Tampa while receiving medical attention.

Benjamin Burnett

Lawrence B. Brown Family

Peter Brown, father: 1810-1885
Catherine Brown, mother: 1818-1923
Lawrence Brown: 9/12/56-6/16/41
Elizabeth Washington: Brown's first wife died 1880s
Laura Lee: Second wife: Divorced 10/12/1897
Annie Belle Granger Brown 5/24/80-9/15/38
Benjamin Burnette, stepson: 5/19/06-2/12/42
Hallie Mae Goodwin, daughter: 12/10/94-3/30/77
Louvenia Brown Thomas, daughter: 9/11/09-2/15/89
Lorenzo Benjamin Brown, son: 10/16/12-4/26/59
Lawrence Clifford Brown, son: 10/24/15-11/12/77
Mary Brown Tugerson, daughter: 6/26/18-9/3/66
Anniebelle Brown, daughter: 9/23/21-9/24/44
Robert E. L. Brown, son: 6/9/24-7/20/2012
Joseph Tugerson, grandson: 12/31/53-8/1/2002

Business Progressions

As indicated on the following ledger page, Brown's business interests flourished and diversified as the twentieth century unfolded. Note that (in the middle of the page) he wrote "stain and varnish" referring to his furniture repair work. The fourth line referred to "glass" and the line above the date 8/30/03 referred to "silvering glass." Both entries concern making mirrors.

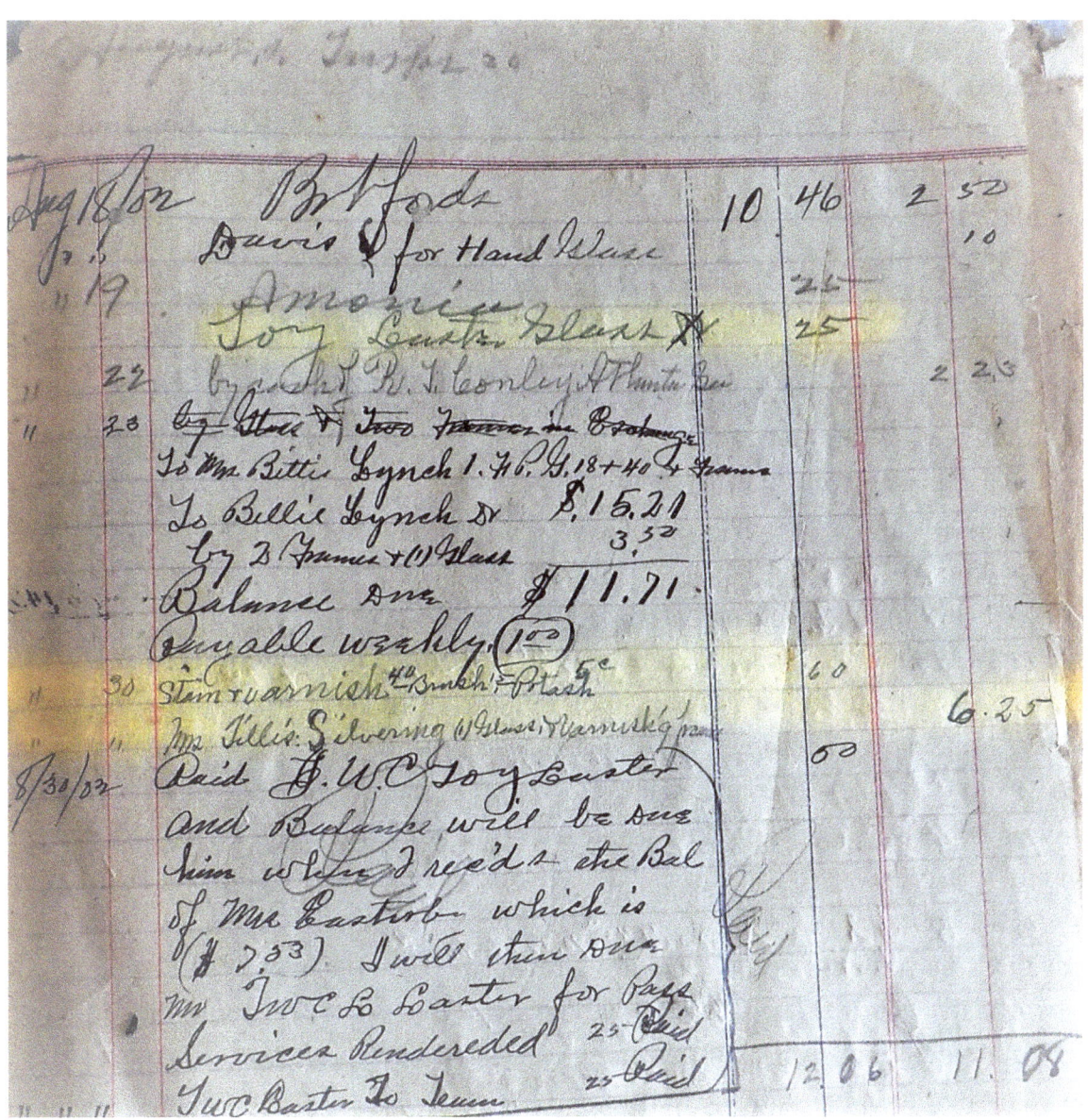

Business Purchases

Racial Tensions Continue Amid Bartow's Progress

As mentioned earlier, racial tensions simmered and occasionally erupted into violence at Bartow into the early 1900s and beyond. In 1909, for instance, arsonists burned the barn of successful black farmer Sam Burkett (grandfather of Lela Burkett, the first black student to receive a high school diploma.) In the 1890s, Burkett was one of the founders of the Burkett Chapple Primitive Baptist Church, which today is a highly regarded religious institution.

During these times of racial troubles, national efforts were started with the goal of bringing the races together. The National Association for the Advancement of Colored People (NAACP) came into existence in 1909. Its mission was "to ensure the political, educational, social, and economic equality of rights of all persons and to eliminate racial hatred and racial discrimination."

Beyond incidents occurring within Brown's home community, instances of racial violence that beset nearby Lakeland and Mulberry touched his life as well. Then, two months after the Burkett arson attack, another Bartow man, accused of assaulting a white woman, was killed when Deputy Frank Scott surrendered Charles Scarborough to a mob. A report noted: "There was no excitement in the matter at all. The people were determined that the negro should pay the penalty for his attempted crime; that was all."

In 1911, Deputy Scott found himself in custody for shooting at an unarmed black chauffeur. The deputy argued to Bartow mayor C. H. Walker that "his intention was only to frighten the negro." Disbelieving, Walker sentenced Scott to a $50.00 fine.[21]

The racial eruptions belied appearances. Canter Brown has written that, during the first decade of the twentieth century, Bartow took quiet pride in itself. "Bartow is a city of homes, not shacks," one reporter commented. Seen as a "democratic" town, racially segregated Bartow had no wealthy section. Well-kept cottages stood next to stately mansions. One observer stated, "Bartow is eminently a city of churches and church-going people," adding that "there is a sentiment of piety amongst the inhabitants that is almost universal and the standard of morality is very high."[22]

Advances did come to Bartow, even though at a slow pace. The town expanded its municipal water works in 1905 with an artesian well that produced water "of unquestionable purity." Voters approved bonds in 1902 to purchase an electric light plant that first opened in 1897. As noted earlier, they chose the Peninsular Telephone Company to bring standard and long-distance telephone service to the town. A $25,000 hotel was built. Named the Hotel Oaks, it was described as a "massive three-story brick structure new in design and construction. Its rooms are all outside rooms. They are steam-heated, electric-lighted, have hot and cold running water in them, some have private baths and there are several public baths in the building. There is no single item wanting to further the comfort of the guest."[23]

In spite of continuing prejudices, some black families managed to thrive. In 1905, 837 black men, women, and children lived in Bartow making up 43 per cent of the total population. Restaurant owner Charles Martin competed directly with whites for business. Some black business people began sending their children to college. In one example, Henry and Dora L. Sweet sent their son William De Vaughn Sweet to Edward Waters College and then to Florida A&M college where he received his master's degree. Another son, Ossian, earned a medical degree.[24]

The automobile first came to Polk County in 1902. While it proved a marvel to look at, many saw it as a nuisance. "Horseless carriages" scared the remaining horses, causing them to scatter. The contraption also raised an awful racket. Cars, though, allowed for more freedom and travel, affording diversions to residents that they would not ordinarily have been able to enjoy.[25]

Significantly, women began emerging more into the public sphere. Polk County's first women's club, organized for white women and called the Smart Set Club, organized in Bartow during 1903.[26]

In the twentieth century's early years, Bartow's outstanding growth eventually began to propel it toward becoming a modern city. Much of the expansion derived from a tendency for more and more area residents to become urban dwellers rather than continue to live in rural areas. A strong economy, led by renewed citrus and phosphate industries, fueled this progress.[27]

Meanwhile, automobiles had become more plentiful by 1907. In that year, seven cars "dash[ed about the streets" and, it was said, "truly Bartow is putting on metropolitan airs." Before the close of the year, fifteen automobiles roamed the community. Some began calling Bartow "the automobile city."[28]

An official census taken in early 1908 reported that the population of Bartow had encompassed 1,691 white persons and 1,200 black citizens, with 178 persons living just outside the city limits. In this same year, a clay road completed between Lakeland and Bartow, afforded easy transportation between those two places.[29]

Optimism flourished along with a growing Polk County economy. The erection of a new courthouse in Bartow symbolized the enthusiasm. One journalist exclaimed, "This temple of justice will be 119 feet 6 inches long by 58 feet wide, three stories and basement in height, and of true classic design. When completed this monument to the thrift and enterprise of Polk County's citizens will have cost $84,000 and when finally furnished the final cost will not be less than $100,000." Dignitaries laid the cornerstone on December 17, 1908. People came from miles around to participate in the huge event.[30]

The year 1909 brought more cause for celebration. On June 1, free delivery of mail began. T. L. Marquis also opened Bartow's first moving picture theater, "The Amusu."[31] Neither of these events, however, could compare to the celebration that had ensued upon completion of the new courthouse.

Louvenia Brown

By way of a personal celebration for the Brown family, Louvenia Catherine Brown was born September 11, 1909. Louvenia was educated in public schools in Bartow and went on to study at Florida Normal and Industrial School (today's Florida Memorial) in St. Augustine and Shaw University in Raleigh, North Carolina.

She married Robert "Bob" Thomas and in 1932 began her teaching career in Bartow at Union Academy. She later taught at Brewster, Florida, in some of the "mine schools." In 1942, Louvenia became coordinator of Veteran's Administration education in Winter Haven. After her divorce, she lived in the Brown House. She remained there alone until her death on February 15, 1989. She was a beloved teacher and contributed importantly to education in Bartow and the surrounding area.

Crowds gathered in Bartow to celebrate completion of Polk County's third courthouse, June 25, 1909. There was a parade of decorated vehicles, a big barbecue, and speeches.

(Polk County Historical Quarterly) Opening of courthouse in 1909.

In 1910, tragically, a fire swept through East Bartow about a block from Brown's residence. The disaster and its aftermath, it should be underscored, illustrated cooperative moments that existed between black citizens and white citizens even during times of racial tension.

The April 21 edition of Bartow's *Courier-Informant*, described the scene. Entitled "Fire Sweeps East Bartow," the piece noted, in part:

> On Sunday afternoon a fire was discovered in a Negro restaurant owned by Charley Macon in East Bartow, having caught from a defective flue and before it could be gotten under control the restaurant and fifteen other Negro houses were destroyed along with the storage tanks and stables of the Standard Oil Company.
>
> A strong wind was blowing and house after house was destroyed, almost without the slightest checking of the flames. The nearest water hydrant was some distance and the pressure was not very good. . . .
>
> . . .the end blew out of the twenty-gallon kerosene tank and a perfect river of oil ran down the hill northward about a hundred yards distance, enveloping the home of Nancy Bell a colored woman. The house was almost new, six rooms, and she had just finished paying for it.
>
> The smoke at this time was so dense and the flames so furious as to beggar description.
>
> …some lost all they had, as we heard one man say that all he had left was what he had on—and he didn't have on a coat or a vest. So it was much harder on the man who lost all he had even small though it was, than the great oil company whose loss was many times as much. But which will not be felt at all."

The following resolution was prepared by victims of the fire:

From the Colored People
Resolution Passed at a Meeting Held Monday Evening

Editor, Courier—Informant:
Dear Sir: In a citizens mass meeting held on Monday evening. April 18, in St. James A. M. E. church for the purpose of electing a relief committee, and otherwise systematizing the work of rendering to the fire suffers of this city, the following resolution was adopted:
Whereas, The colored citizens of East Bartow have suffered one of the greatest calamities in the history of the town, in the recent fire of the 17th inst., which reduced to ashes almost the entire business section, and
Whereas, The white people have rendered such timely assistance, using every means in their power to aid in saving our property, therefore Resolved, That we

FROM SLAVERY TO COMMUNITY BUILDER

adopt this method to show our thanks and appreciation for the heroic service rendered us, in our time of need. That such kindness will not be forgotten, and if the opportunity ever offers under like circumstances we will willingly do our part to the best of our ability.

Resolved, Further that we request the publication of these resolutions in the Courier—Informant.

C. C. Johnson, Chairman

C. E. Murray, Secretary

Brown's Thrifty Nature

Through high and low times, Lawrence Brown continued to study and learn. In doing so, he tended to measure and calculate almost everything. For instance, a large peanut farm operated across from his home. As can be seen from the following journal entry, he measured and studied the growing peanuts.

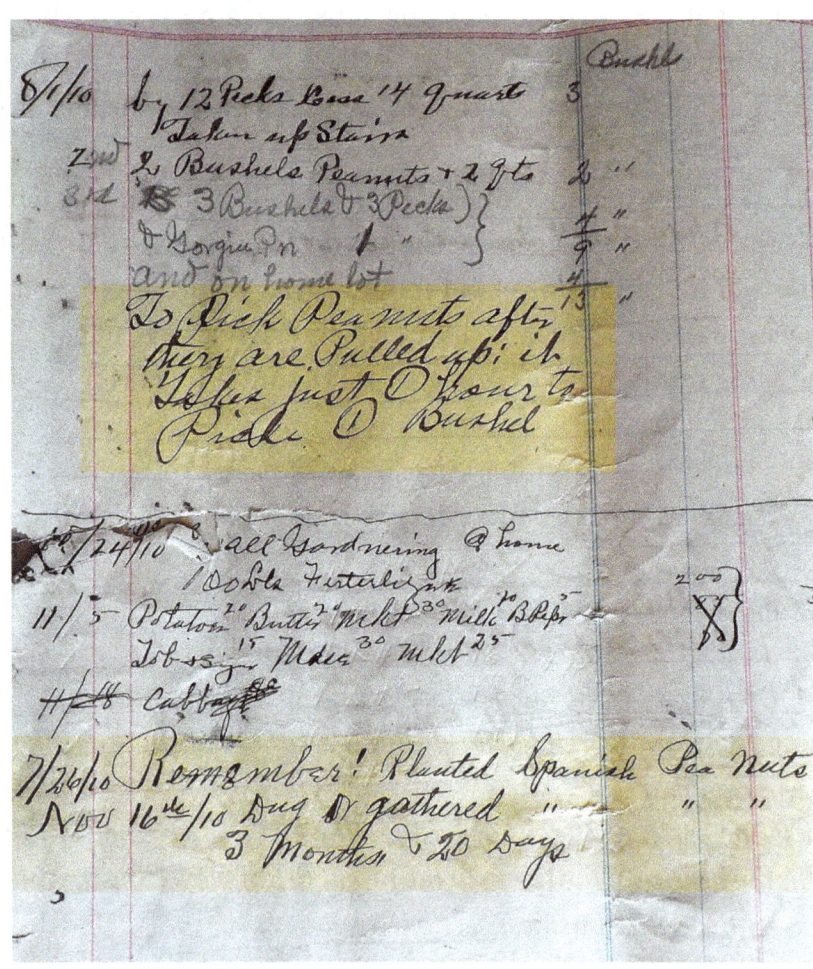

Peanuts

To pick peanuts after they are pulled up: it takes just 1 hour to pick 1 bushel
7/26/10 Remember! Planted Spanish Peanuts
Nov. 16th/10 Dug or gathered "   "
                                    3 months & 20 days

Stolen Shotgun

The journal entry seen here is interesting for what it does not tell us. Its author clearly knew how to keep his secrets, when he considered discretion necessary. Brown knew who had stolen his shotgun. Still, he did not report how he handled that fact. We do not know if he went to the sheriff, confronted the men, or ever got his gun back. He knew, of course, it would have been dangerous to approach the sheriff if the thieves happened to be white men.

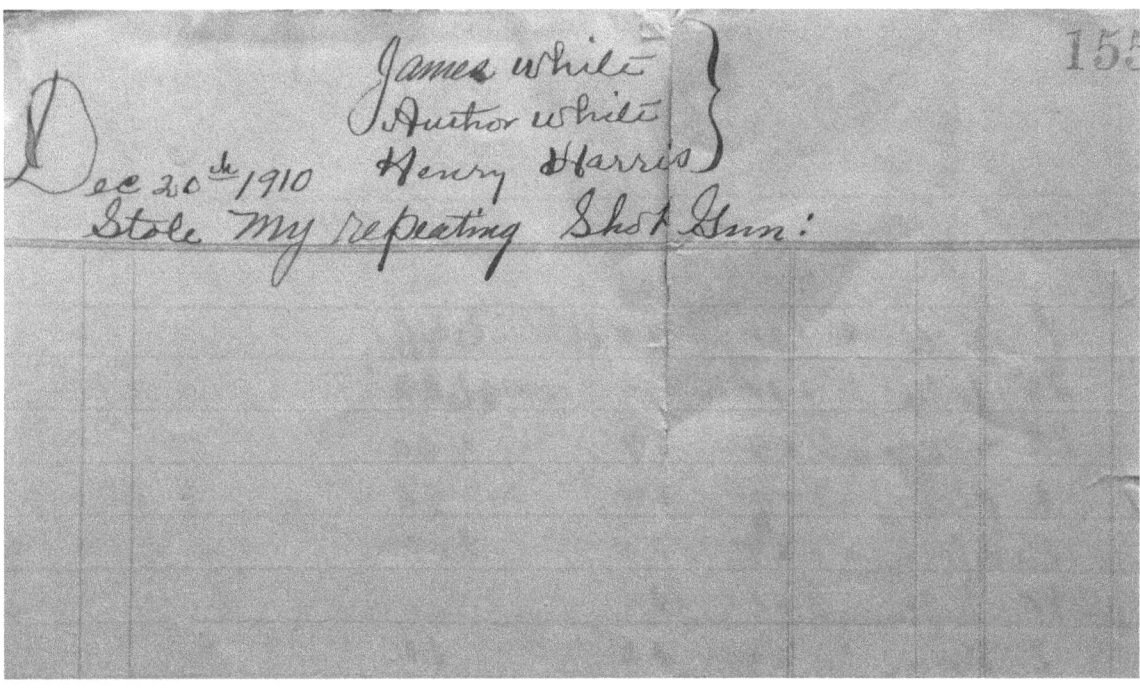

Range of Influence

Brown's range of contacts and, to some extent, his influence extended to the whole community. His businesses contributed to the city's economic growth. On one occasion, to cite a pertinent example, he spent $1000 on building materials and other merchandise, much of these expenditures going to white merchants.

More Thrifty Nature

L. B. Brown's ledgers demonstrate his organizational skills, curiosity, and thrifty nature. His inquisitiveness led him to question whether purchasing pork from the local butcher would be more economical than raising and slaughtering his own pigs. The following page shows his calculations to find an answer. At the top of the page is the cost per pound to raise a pig:

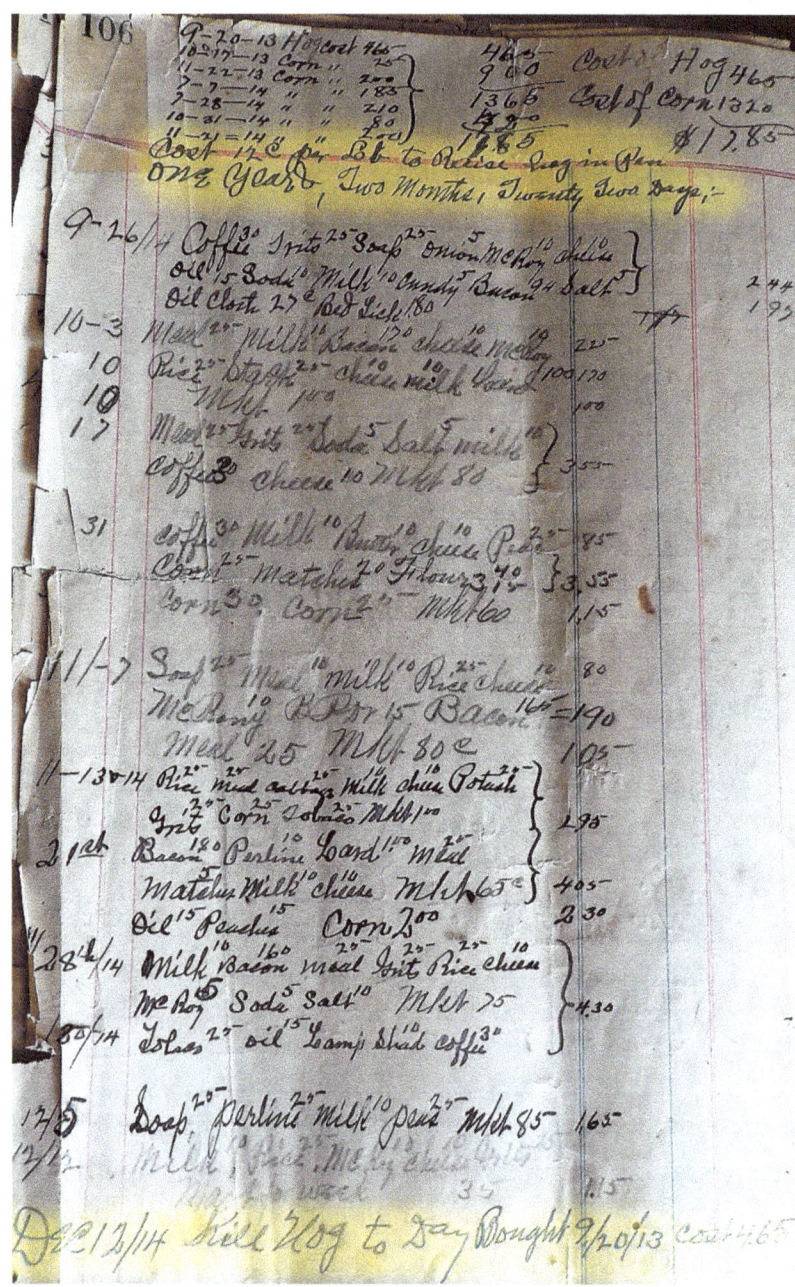

Brown's Thrifty Nature

Cost 12 cents per lb. to raise pig in pen
One year, two months, twenty two days

He had raised the pig for one year, two months and twenty-two days. The last line specifies when he bought it, when he killed it, and how much the animal cost him.

Lorenzo Brown

Annie Belle and Lawrence's second child, Lorenzo Benjamin, was born on October 16, 1912. He was a teacher until polio rendered him bedridden. He died April 26, 1959. Lorenzo is the adult in the photo.

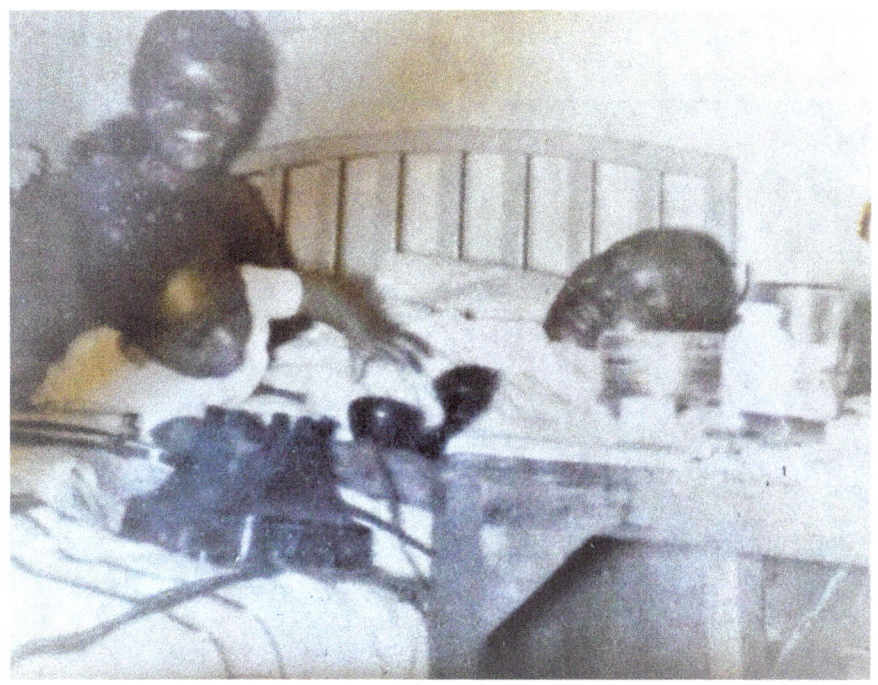

Lorenzo Brown. The identity of the young woman and baby are not known.

Brown and Bartow, 1914 to 1919

The year 1914 brought Bartow prosperity and a range of local improvements. The town constructed $130,000 worth of new paving, and spent $40,000 to enlarge the city-owned light and water plant, $25,000 for additional sewerage, $8,000 for a public library building, $5,000 for a motor driven fire-fighting apparatus, and—at the end of the year—prepared to spend

$125,000 more on street paving. Additionally, the city council bought the old jail building from the county.[32]

In spite of the improvements, Bartow's atmosphere differed from that found in other prosperous locales. Modest growth and loss of its premier status among Polk County towns imposed a more restrained tone. Excitement connected with building and construction elsewhere contrasted sharply with Bartow's reserve.

With respect to healthcare, a number of individuals within the black community offered critical leadership. Dr. Ledge Wynn McNeill, for example, had established a medical practice in 1912 that offered medical care at a modest cost for persons throughout the county.[33] Within two years, his medical college training elevated him high on the list of qualified physicians within Polk. White patients likely already availed themselves of his skills, while black sufferers delighted in his presence. Black women served in the important function as midwives for black and white women, assisting them in giving birth, until 1916 when Bartow's first hospital was built.

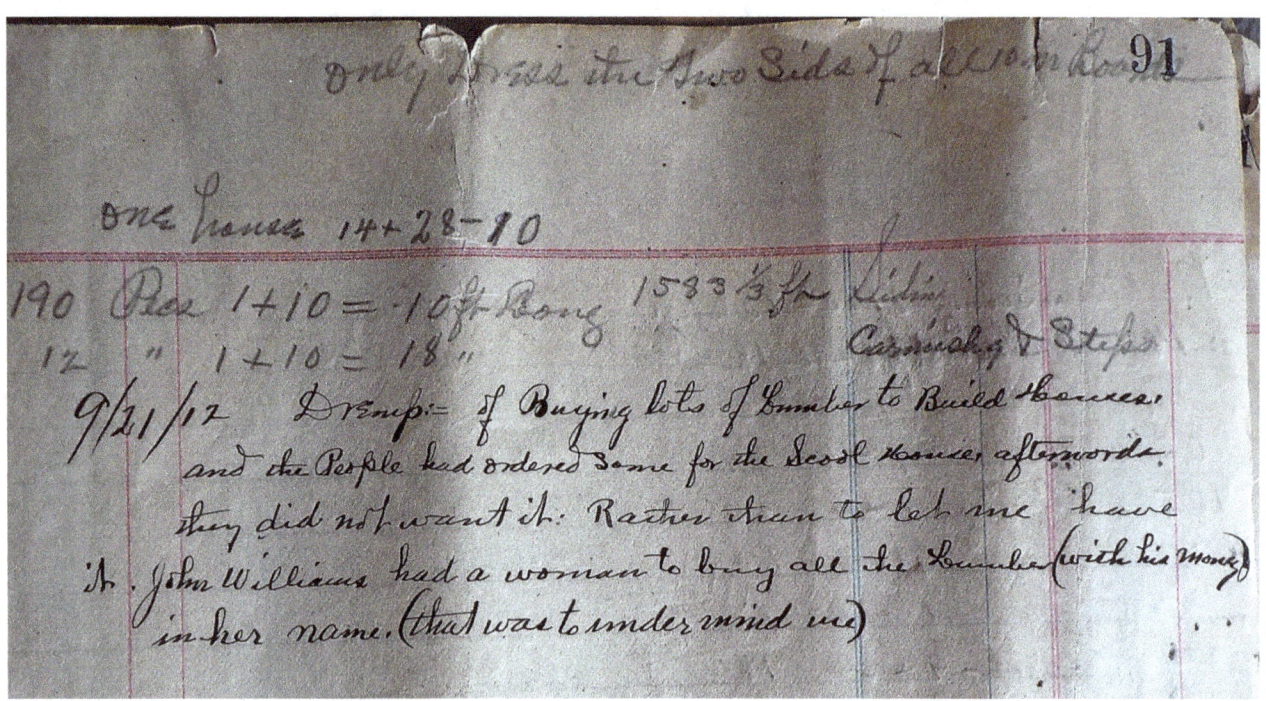

Sometimes Brown would record his dreams in his journals. This is an example of one of his dreams. Perhaps it represents some of the difficulties he faced in the community.

9/21/12 Dremp: of Buying lots of Lumber to Build Houses and the people had ordered some for the Scool House afterwards they did not want it. Rather than to let me have it, John Williams had a woman to buy all the lumber (with his money) in her name. (that was to undermind me.)

Annie Belle Brown's Involvement in the Business

Annie's activities on behalf of her husband's business interests to some extent confounded customs of the era. Women generally found themselves excluded from participation in their spouse's business and financial matters during this time period. Lawrence, however, included his wife in the family business. Underscoring her situation, Annie Belle also enjoyed the distinction of maintaining her own bank account. Her ability to handle real estate transactions and to manage a checking account indicates that she was an educated woman.

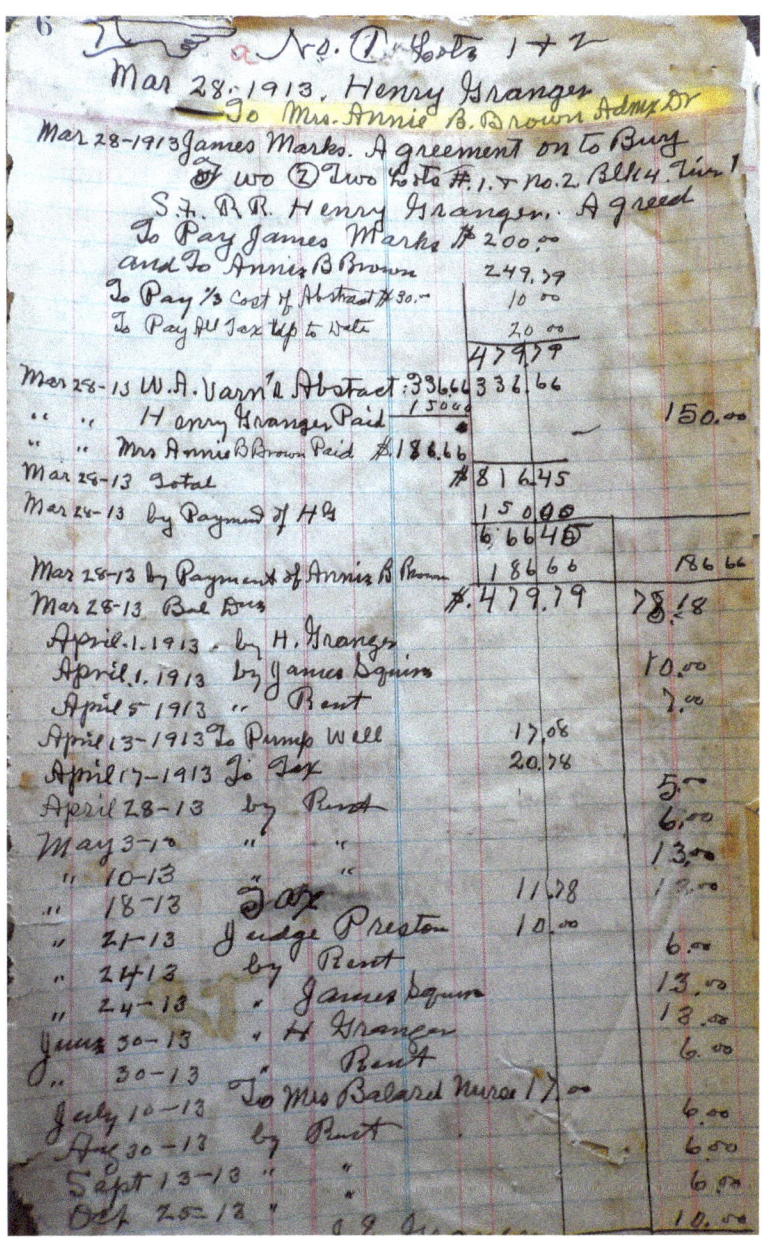

This ledger illustrates the involvement of Lawrence's wife Annie Bell in their business.

As the Browns worked together to build their business success, the spirit of patriotism ran high. Thousands celebrated July 4, 1914, at Bartow, making the festivities the largest gathering in Polk County to that time. The event featured an automobile parade, baseball games, and a barbecue. A "flying machine" demonstration unfortunately did not go well. The new-fangled contraption barely cleared ten feet off the ground.

Automobiles became more numerous during the era, which increasingly led to a major problem. Good roads had become a dire necessity. Rain, it turned out, washed away the much vaunted "Bartow clay." Portions of the electorate expressed little interest, however, in approving what they considered to be extravagant outlays. They wanted to explore cheap alternatives such as "sand-oil" roads. Fortunately, the Polk County Good Roads Association—a group made up of influential Bartow men—set forth a plan to interconnect the county's towns with asphalt highways. By 1919, their goal had been accomplished.

Financial prosperity soon suffered from a terrible international conflict. In August 1914, war broke out in Europe. The conflict caused local economic hardships. Phosphate sales declined and some mines closed when industry income fell by 20 per cent. Although the citrus and cattle industries suffered difficulties as well, the setbacks injured, but failed to destroy the local economy.

Understandably, though, the area's boom slowed as an inflationary spiral cut the dollar's value in half from 1914 to 1919. Many residents soon left rural areas to settle in urban locales. Bartow's population increased by about one-fourth.[34]

Aiding the changes, transportation innovations continued to appear. As "good roads" were built, railroads, too, implemented upgrades. By 1917, Bartow boasted three railroad stations to service passengers and freight.[35]

Birth of Lawrence Clifford Brown

As Bartow grew, so did the Brown family. Annie gave birth to third child Lawrence Clifford Brown on October 24, 1915. He ultimately married Dewey Livingston on December 28, 1940. He and his wife spent their entire married life in Lakeland. Typical of Lawrence and Annie's children, he participated actively in the community through several organizations. He served as deacon and trustee of the First Baptist Institutional Church and, for 35 years, presided as superintendent of the church Sunday school. He also contributed as an officer in the Polk County Teachers Credit Union and served on several committees for the city of Lakeland. A member of the Armed Forces during World War II, he taught at Jewett High School in Winter Haven before becoming director of athletics at Washington Parks High School and then at Rochelle Senior High School. He eventually led Rochelle Elementary School as principal. Subsequently, he served as assistant principal at Kathleen High School. He died November 9, 1977.

Lawrence Clifford Brown

World War I

Toddler Lawrence Clifford Brown was beginning to explore the world around him when danger neared Bartow on a grand scale. In the early months of 1917, the U. S. moved closer to joining the fighting in Europe. Soon, German submarines sank five American merchant ships and President Wilson urged Congress to declare war. In May, the Selective Service Act required young men to sign-up for the armed forces.

The war effort produced many new programs and propelled the growth of old ones: "victory gardens" sprouted in the yards of many homes and Red Cross programs afforded residents another option for aiding in the effort. Boys' and girls' programs such as Boy Scouts and Camp Fire Girls, as well as newly organized groups of Victor Boys and Victor Girls, helped to raise needed funds.

Unfortunately, not even the war effort stemmed the ongoing tide of racist behavior. In particular, some white people spread rumors that African Americans were not doing their part in the war effort. Nothing could be further from the truth, and examples could be found at every hand. The Colored Red Cross Society worked hard, to name just one. Tuskegee Institute graduate George H. Mays, Jr. served as a leader in the black communities to raise money. By August 22, 1918, reports confirmed that of 1,193 Polk Countians in the service, 575 were black. News of the war's progress in fact, often came through letters home from servicemen overseas.

On November 11, 1918, word of the war's end finally brought elation to the country, but celebrations were muted due to a pandemic outbreak of Spanish influenza. By Christmas, most had returned from Europe. Yet, they encountered at home threat of illness or even death.[36] Black health care professionals, including Dr. McNeill, labored to care for black and white patients. Many owed their lives to the courage and kindness of those men and women.

Returning veterans naturally desired to maintain bonds forged during their military service. In these circumstances the American Legion was born. Its posts often bore the names of deceased veterans. The Bartow chapter honored Giddings Oglesby; for black servicemen, the city of Lakeland named its black branch Alex Brown Post No. 175.

Birth of Mary Brown

Mary Brown Tugerson

Five months before the war's end, Annie Belle gave birth to Mary on June 26, 1918. Mary graduated Junior High School from Union Academy in May 1934. She married Joseph Tugerson and gave Lawrence and Annie Belle their only grandchild, Joseph Tugerson. Mary died September 3, 1966.

Sometimes, conflicts arose to confront returned servicemen. In Europe, they had witnessed customs and patterns of life that stood at odds with more conservative Bartow lifestyles. In April 1919, famous evangelist Billy Sunday preached to a Bartow crowd of six to seven thousand people. Utilizing his famed emotionally powerful style, he demanded the eradication of sinful ways and deeds. Other preachers picked up Sunday's message decrying gambling and "rotten pictures" shown in local movie theatres.

Other patterns of life—most particularly political ones—remained static. Influential individuals and business concerns kept white control of elections thanks to a poll tax that allowed only the financially well-off to vote. At times, a business owner paid his employees' tax so they could vote, of course, for the man the owner supported.[37]

Phosphate mines continued to furnish work for many local men. Black workers made up about 95 percent of the labor force. All foremen were white. From the early 1900s, the average worker had earned $2.50 per day, plus board, in a company-provided house in exchange for 10 to 12-hour days, six days per week.

In 1919, workers' union representatives demanded a minimum wage of 37 cents an hour and eight-hour days. All 17 area phosphate companies refused the bid. In April, the workers struck. When companies imported out-of-state replacement workers, violence erupted. Despite the presence of the National Guard, the troubles continued. "Scab" workers, phosphate security guards, a deputy, and a toddler, among others, died in the ensuing conflict.

Finally, in September a federal judge issued a restraining order against the union, and federal marshals began riding the phosphate trains. The violence ended. Workers returned to the mines in October. They received a settlement of 10-hour shifts for $3 per day.[38]

When phosphate mines opened in Southern Polk County, most of the laborers were black while all the foremen were white.

Photo courtesy of the Lakeland Ledger

Painful Parting at the L. B. Brown House

Lawrence's mother, Catherine, died on March 14, 1923, at 5:25 p.m. Her last words to Lawrence were:

You must work less at night and rest more in the day.

Loved ones buried her at Glenwood, Florida, on March 18. Her remains later were brought to Bartow, where she now lies in the family burial plot in Evergreen Cemetery.

Lawrence's mother, Catherine

The Twenties Bring Changes and Challenges

Writer Scott Fitzgerald labeled the 1920s the "Jazz Age" thus indelibly characterizing the period for future generations. The nation partied in the aftermath of unimaginable wartime loss. Sooner or later, though, the price for that heady experience was sure to come due.

In 1920, the Eighteenth Amendment prohibiting the consumption of intoxicants became law. Although Bartow had been "dry" in a legal sense for most of the time since the 1880s, moonshine could be purchased readily. With Prohibition, alcohol consumption skyrocketed. Members of government looked the other way or accepted bribes as the "Roaring" Twenties rankled many conservative residents.

Also, at the decade's beginning, in August 1920, and following many rallies and much individual suffering, the Nineteenth Amendment passed giving women the right to vote. "Thousands of African-American women were active in the suffrage movement, addressing issues of race, gender, and class, as well as enfranchisement, often through the church but eventually through organizations devoted to specific causes. While white women sought the vote to gain an equal voice in the political process, African-American women often sought the vote as a means of racial uplift and as a way to effect change in the post-Reconstruction era. Notable African-American suffragists such as Mary Church Terrell, Sojourner Truth, Frances Ellen Watkins Harper, Fannie Barrier Williams, and Ida B. Wells-Barnett advocated for suffrage in tandem with civil rights for African-Americans."[39] Unfortunately, in spite of their efforts, black women did not get to vote at this time.

The Nineteenth Amendment stated: "The right of citizens of the United States to vote shall not be denied or abridged by the United States or by any State on account of sex."

In the 1920s, the nation also entered a period of enthusiastic economic expansion. Bartow shared in this growth. In one measure, the revenue for building permits increased from $132,569 in 1922 to over $1,000,000 by 1925. The local population grew from 4,203 in 1920 to 6,000 by 1924. Building construction in commercial and residential districts surged.[40]

Birth of Annie Belle Brown

Anniebelle Brown

Annie Belle, Lawrence and Annie Belle's fifth child was born September 23, 1921. Never having married, she died September 24, 1944.

By 1922, innovations in communication were advancing rapidly. The invention of the radio broke down regional barriers and encouraged residents to think beyond their narrow boundaries. And, on February 5, the automatic telephone system began operation in Bartow. At that time, 545 phones were in use.

Women's styles changed. When Charles Earnest arranged a fashion show highlighting styles of the past, he learned that lesson immediately. The eighteen-and nineteen-inch waist of the Victorian era, it became clear, no longer represented the typical woman's body type.

Other events also grated on moral critics. For example, progressive education such as Charles Darwin's theories of evolution challenged cherished beliefs, causing many to be dismayed. Whether the theory could ever be taught in public schools posed a question that stirred local passions and raised hackles.

The high living of the Twenties sparked a further reaction with the resurgence of the Ku Klux Klan. This group claimed to represent seeking a return to Protestant, "American" values. Its support for "100% Americanism" masked negative attitudes toward anyone who was not a white, Anglo-Saxon, Protestant. Racist attitudes lay behind KKK murders of several black men for "annoying" white women.[41]

The price came due beginning in mid-1926. When the economic crash took place, many in Bartow and the rest of Polk County believed the collapse would not affect them. In the first half of 1926, building in Bartow matched the pace of the previous years. However, by October, Bartow authorities had cut their 1927 budget estimate by 25 per cent. The town lost 6 percent of its population between 1925 and 1930.

Relative stability in citrus and phosphate industries helped the area endure this rough period. Because these industries continued to do well, the African American community fared better than the white community during the Bust. African American professional men and merchants survived as well. Remaining open were Fred Waldon's grocery store; the Robinson funeral parlor; Thomas Franklin Burnett's men's and women's apparel emporium (he was the younger brother of Benjamin Burnett, Annie Bell's first husband); the movie theater; and the "Blue Room" dance hall.

Resident Charlie McNeil, the only child of Dr. Ledge McNeil, Bartow's first black doctor, reflected on the times, stating banks refused to loan money to African Americans. She continued: "Colored folks became self-supporting, building for present needs and becoming worthwhile citizens of Bartow and Polk County. None were college men having completed business studies in economics, or having ever heard of business seminars. They were just plain folks with tenacity to obtain economic stability for themselves and their families while supplying the needs of their community with what existed at the time."

The prosperity of the 1920s brought improved public resources for African American families in Bartow. Rising land values allowed the construction of new and better schools for black children, though the low levels of government support never allowed them to match the standards for white children. Churches benefited as well. Mt. Gilboa Baptist Church, for one, reconstructed its building in stone.[42]

Birth of Robert E. L. Brown

Annie Belle gave birth to Robert E. L. Brown on January 5, 1924. He was the last child born to Annie Belle and Lawrence. Robert worked on the Pennsylvania Railroad as a Pullman Porter, acquiring skills in food preparation. His talents led the owner of the railroad to ask that Robert be assigned to his private car. After retiring from the railroad, Robert moved to New York where he worked for New York City's Department of Corrections, eventually being promoted to the position of Director of Food Service operations. Robert died July 20, 2012. Fortunately, he lived during the early years of the restoration of his boyhood home and was able to share his memories of those times. He contributed artifacts and contributed financially towards the restoration project. He is buried in Evergreen Cemetery in Bartow.

By early 1926, L. B. Brown took pride that he owed no one a single penny. However, with the end of the Florida boom that year, this situation changed dramatically. His housing business and family illness soon saddled him with obligations that resulted in financial struggles. Meanwhile, Bartow had begun installing sewers and requiring houses to install indoor plumbing connected to the city's system. Brown undertook installation of thirty-three toilets as well as satisfying increased county taxes and insurance costs. Still, he generated sufficient funds to purchase paint and hire skilled workers to paint all of his houses.

Robert E. L. Brown

On top of these expenses, Brown covered tuition and other expenses for Ben's Jacksonville boarding school and Lavenia's costs for schooling at St. Augustine. He meanwhile was compelled to face the fact that his wife had become very sick. In October 1926, she traveled by ambulance to the Clara Frye Hospital in Tampa. She could not move her arms, stand up, or turn herself in bed. She remained in the hospital from October 31 to December 18. "When she returned," he happily recorded, "she could stand up and walk a little."

This 1930 Census page shows that Lawrence and Annie had four children living with them: Clifford, Mary, Annie, and Robert. Benjamin, Lorenzo, and Louvenia lived elsewhere.

The Great Depression

Three years or so after the Florida Bust, the nation entered upon the Great Depression with the stock market crash that commenced in October 1929. Polk's diverse economy continued to offer security for many, but real want confronted many households in every area including Bartow.

The Klan meanwhile remained a major factor in Polk through the 1930s, opposing racial intermingling and supporting violence as a bloody tool.[43] In addition to its work of monitoring moral behaviors, the KKK continued to broadcast a message of hate and religious intolerance. Many white citizens rejected the teachings of the Klan, and some actively opposed them. Klan vigilante work unfortunately often had the support of law enforcement officers. The violence, usually directed at black citizens, could also reach any white person who openly opposed them.

Despite these dangerous times, Lawrence Brown persisted, using his personal skills to thrive and keep his family safe. During these difficult times, Lawrence strove to care for the poor and contributed generously to his neighbors. His daughter Lavonia wrote:

When hog killing time came, from four to five swine would be killed. Neighbors and friends would come from afar to help. He had a smokehouse. The doors of our house were never locked, the smokehouse was left open. Anything neighbors and friends needed they would come by and tell either the mother, the grandmother or our poppa what they needed; they were welcome to supply their needs.

Beginning in 1933, President Roosevelt's "New Deal" promised financial help for communities and jobs for their citizens. The Work Projects Administration helped the city with road and municipal services improvements and with the construction of a civic center and an armory. Black residents enjoyed some employment opportunities and other benefits, but most were secured by white residents.[44]

Chronic problems continued in Polk even as times improved. Two issues stood out: election irregularities and corrupt law enforcement. Many residents held intense concerns about widespread illegal gambling and bootleg liquor. Meanwhile, crime and violence rates surged.

A few bright spots shone through. In a major move, Bartow State Senator Spessard Holland and State Senator Ernest Graham of Miami pushed for the repeal of the poll tax in Florida that had kept many from being able to vote, placing elections in the hands of a few powerful men.

And, in 1935, a case against a group of Klansmen and a number of law enforcement officers gained national attention. The trial was moved from Hillsborough County to Bartow due to the recusal of the Tampa judge and the tense atmosphere there. The floggings and lynching in question seemed aimed at stopping union organizing efforts. The nation watched the proceedings with interest to see what kind of justice would be handed out by a southern white jury in Polk County. The guilty verdict surprised everyone and became a turning point in Florida justice.

There were bumps along the road. A national economic downturn in 1938 caused tax collections to plummet, greatly reducing money available for schools. To make do with their reduced income, the school board let many employees go, cut teachers' salaries, and shortened the school year. Tragically, in 1939 Germany invaded Poland bringing about the beginning of World War II. The war devastated the local phosphate industry as Germany had been its primary customer.[45]

The year 1938 proved a difficult one for Lawrence Brown personally with the death of his beloved wife Annie. Nevertheless, during this time the 83-year-old Brown maintained support for his community. As Bartow resident and local historian Lloyd Harris noted: "Mt. Zion A.M.E. Church held its first services in the home of L. B. Brown beginning September 1936 until the church was erected in 1937 on Palmetto St. Fire destroyed the church in Sept 1938. Services were again held in L. B. Brown's home until the completion of the new church. Its first service was held on Jan 1, 1939."

Robert Brown, the youngest of Lawrence and Annie's children, recalled the times vividly. He informed interviewer Clifton Lewis that as a child he fetched eggs from under the house where hens had laid them. He remarked, as well, that the family did not use the water well. Instead, they drew from the water pump near the back porch. He recalled his father being strict, but kind. "He was very tall," Robert added, "about 6 feet 3 or 4 inches." Robert was the only child of Lawrence and Annie Bell not to attend college. Rather, as mentioned earlier, he elected to secure a good paying job in Jacksonville working for the railroad as a Pullman porter.

Robert E. L. Brown, left, last surviving child of Lawrence and Annie Belle Brown, with Clifton Lewis of the NIC in Bartow.

FROM SLAVERY TO COMMUNITY BUILDER

Lawrence Bernard Brown died on June 16, 1941 at the age of eighty-five. The *Polk County Record* edition published Friday, June 17, reported on page one:

L. B. Brown, one of the first colored settlers to reside in Bartow, passed away at his home in Bartow Thursday at 7:30 AM.

He was well known in Bartow, having operated a furniture store for many years and owned a considerable amount of property in the colored East side section of Bartow.

Brown is survived by his seven children and a number of other relatives in Bartow.

Funeral services will be held at Mt. Gilboa Baptist Church Sunday, January 19th.

Historian Canter Brown observed of him: "Lawrence B. Brown's life and accomplishments testify to his character, wisdom, and skills. Born into slavery and emancipated only with the Civil War's end, he lived afterward in times that became increasingly dangerous for Black men." Brown added: "Lawrence Bernard Brown commanded respect. An outstanding black businessman and community leader, he helped to build modern Florida. Sadly, history books have not told Brown's story or those of countless similar African American men and women. For too long, tales of individuals who refused to yield to the injustice of discrimination and oppression were considered too dangerous to society because they might undercut the customs of everyday life in a racially segregated world. Today, Brown's saga must be told. It inspires. It provokes thought. And, it stands as a fitting reminder of fine men and women history has forgotten but who made a difficult world a much better place in which to live."

Lawrence B. Brown September 12, 1856—June 16, 1941

Grave of Lawrence Bernard Brown in Bartow, Florida

The United States of America,

TO ALL TO WHOM THESE PRESENTS SHALL COME, GREETING:

Homestead Certificate No. 2060
Application 712

Whereas, there has been deposited in the GENERAL LAND OFFICE of the United States a CERTIFICATE of the Register of the Land Office at Gainesville Florida, whereby it appears that, pursuant to the Act of Congress approved 20th May, 1862, "To secure Homesteads to actual settlers on the public domain," and the acts supplemental thereto, the claim of Peter Brown has been established and duly consummated in conformity to law for the south-east quarter of the south-east quarter of section thirty-two, in township eleven south of range eighteen east of Tallahassee Meridian, in Florida, containing thirty-nine acres and four hundredths of an acre according to the Official Plat of the Survey of the said Land returned to the GENERAL LAND OFFICE by the SURVEYOR GENERAL.

Now know ye, That there is therefore granted by the UNITED STATES, unto the said Peter Brown the tract of Land above described: TO HAVE AND TO HOLD the said tract of Land, with the appurtenances thereof, unto the said Peter Brown and to his heirs and assigns forever.

In Testimony whereof, I, Chester A. Arthur, PRESIDENT OF THE UNITED STATES OF AMERICA, have caused these letters to be made Patent, and the SEAL OF THE GENERAL LAND OFFICE to be hereunto affixed.

Given under my hand, at the CITY OF WASHINGTON, the twenty-fifth day of August, in the year of Our Lord one thousand eight hundred and eighty-two, and of the Independence of the United States the one hundred and seventh.

By the President: Chester A. Arthur

By O. L. Judd Asst., Sec'y.
S. W. Clark, Recorder of the General Land Office.

1882 Homestead Certificate of Peter Brown
The Homestead Act of 1862 allowed any head of household or adult 21 years of age, to claim 160 acres if they lived on the land for five continuous years, built a home on it, made improvements, and had never borne arms against the U. S.

(4—070.)

HOMESTEAD PROOF.

Final Affidavit Required of Homestead Claimants.

SECTION 2291 OF THE REVISED STATUTES OF THE UNITED STATES.

I, Peter Brown, having made a Homestead entry of the S E¼ of S E¼ Section No. 32 in Township No. 11 S of Range No. 18 E, subject to entry at Gainesville, Fla. under section No. 2289 of the Revised Statutes of the United States, do now apply to perfect my claim thereto by virtue of section No. 2291 of the Revised Statutes of the United States; and for that purpose do solemnly Swear that I am a citizen of the United States; that I have made actual settlement upon and have cultivated said land, having resided thereon since the 4th day of June, 1874 to the present time; that no part of said land has been alienated, except as provided in section 2288 of the Revised Statutes, but that I am the sole *bona fide* owner as an actual settler; that I will bear true allegiance to the Government of the United States; and further, that I have not heretofore perfected or abandoned an entry made under the homestead laws of the United States. + that I could not appear on this 4th Oct. on account of sickness + his and that I could bring but one witness old reumed + am therefore obliged to sub-
stitute Mr. S.F. Halladay

Peter X Brown
   mark

I, John F. Rollins, Receiver, of the Land Office at Gainesville, Fla., do hereby certify that the above affidavit was subscribed and sworn to before me this 5th day of Oct., 1880

I also certify that no one appeared to object to Peter Brown's proof

John F. Rollins

Electros.

Peter Brown's Final Affidavit of Homestead

MEMORANDUM

Aug. 22nd 1897 Acquainted & went for Lunch & Disported

Bartow Polk Co., Fla.

Laura Lee & L.B. Brown United in the Holy Bond of Marriage Sept. 8th 7.30 Pm 1897

Laura Brown + L.B. Brown Parted on the 12th (Twelth) day of Oct. 10.30 Pm 1897

(1) One Month; (5) Five Days; and (3) Three Hours. To the minute

Oct. 17th Laura B. Returned at 7.30 Pm

January — 1898

June 12th ____ Kneejoke child born 1877

June 13 ____ Amede Plagous — Baptised ____

(Oct. 1st 1897, Atonshioni:) 3.22th 28th — or at 4.15 P.m. washing came to home

8=25=1898. ____ left at 9 oclock A.M.

Jo. 30th & 11th & 2nd 1899 Laura Stayed over all knight

9=28. ____ took hold of my arm ____

____ ____ Came to no ____ 9=30=9 ____

with ____ in the Ap.

Mary Brown Confessed Religion 8/13/1933

Lavine Catherine Brown to Thomas Oct. 1934

Annie Bell Converted Baptised Aug 25 1930

L.B. Brown Converted May 11-1892 ____ 9-7-84

Baptised May 28=1882 ____ 9-28-19

Lavinia B. Brown Converted Baptised June 21 abo. 2 Pm 1925

Robert Lee Brown Converted Baptised Aug. 20. 1935

Note the first two lines announce L. B. Brown's marriage to Laura Lee and the next four announce the end of their marriage "To the minute." Mr. Brown seems to have been happy to dissolve this marriage due to her harsh treatment of his mother.

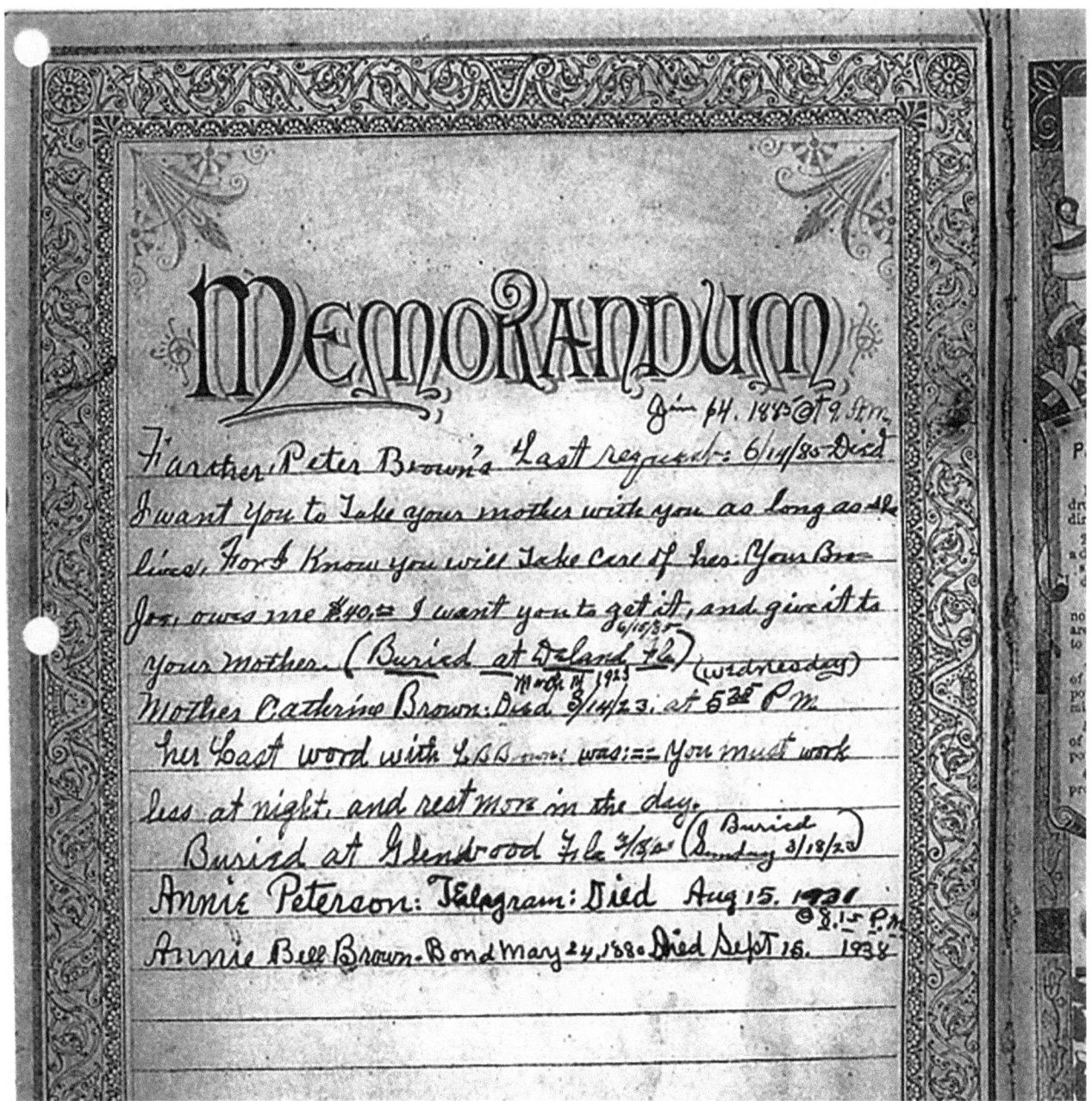

This page from the family Bible shows L. B. Brown's record of his father's last words to him as well as his mother's last words to him. Mr. Brown completed his father's request by caring for his mother until her death in 1923.

BIRTHS

Lavinia Catherine Brown (Garrett) @ 5:00 A.m. Jan 11th 1910
Lorenzo Benjamine Brown (Wilson) at 12 Pm to ½ Pass 12 P.m. 10/16/12
Lawrence Clifford A Brown Oct 24th 1915 @ 4 Pm d Garrett
Benjamine D Burnett May 19, 1906 Garrett (4/3½ 18½ lbs)
Annie B Brown May 24, 1880
Mary Magdalene Brown (Wilson) June 26th at 6½ Am 1918
Annie Bell Brown Sept 23rd 1921 @ 9:30 Pm
Robert Lee Brown Jan 9 1924
L B Brown Sept 12 1856

A page from the family Bible showing Lawrence Brown's children and his own date of birth.

Funeral Services

For

Sister Annie Bell Brown

To Be Held At

ST. JAMES A. M. E. CHURCH

Sunday, September 18, 1938

at 2:30 P. M.

PROGRAM

1. Processional.
2. Hymn, "Come Ye Disconsolate" .... Rev. S. A. Thomas
3. Prayer .... Rev. D. Hill
4. Selection .... Choir
5. Scripture Lesson .... Rev. A. L. Washington
6. Solo, "I've Done My Work" .... Sister L. M. Longworth
7. Sister Brown As a Christian .... Bro. G. W. Anthony
8. Hymn, "Servant of God Well Done"..Rev. S. P. Haynes
9. Obituary .... G. Fogartie
10. Favorite Song, "He's The Joy of My Salvation"
    .... Bro. W. Richardson
11. Eulogy .... Rev. S. C. Sasser
12. Recessional.

Program from Annie Bell Brown's funeral service

Joseph Tugerson, Mary Brown's son
December 31, 1953—August 1, 2002

Chapter 3

The L. B. Brown House/Museum

L. B. Brown, by then a respected builder and contractor in Bartow, erected his comfortable two-story home in 1892. It quickly emerged as a focal point for residents of East Bartow, signifying the local black prosperity of the late nineteenth century. Black Bartowans—and, doubtless, more than a few white residents—admired the Queen Anne-influenced, Victorian "gingerbread" house, a style of architecture commonly utilized and appreciated during that era.[1]

On a more personal level, the house held special significance for Lawrence and Annie as all of their children were born there. As was common for the times, midwives facilitated the birth process. Fortunately, Lawrence had conceived a design that accommodated a large family. The four bedrooms, living room, dining room, kitchen, and bath allowed the family to live comfortably.

Intricate millwork, playful gingerbread trim, and outstanding craftsmanship throughout evidenced Brown's carpentry skills. These special decorative touches encouraged a real sense of home for the family. Because the structure's foundation consisted of southern pine tree stumps, some residents called the home "the house that grew out of trees."

Louvenia Brown Thomas, Lawrence and Annie's first child, happily recalled the early house and grounds. Especially, she remembered fruit trees, grape arbors, pecan trees, oaks, and a large vegetable garden that surrounded the home in its heyday. One drawback, however, came to her mind. The house originally boasted no inside bathrooms, she recollected. Rather, family members resorted to the use of "outhouses." This was common as recent as the 1940s when half of the homes did not have indoor plumbing for showers and toilets. The percentage of homes without these conveniences was higher in African-American neighbors because their areas did not have sewer lines until well after white neighborhoods.

Brown built his home before electric power became available at Bartow. Typically, the family utilized oil lamps and large china lamps for lighting. A wood stove provided their cooking appliance. Food was kept cool in an ice box with a galvanized interior.

The Browns, as did many neighbors, routinely welcomed travelers to their home. It particularly served local people as a resting stop when they were traveling between uptown and downtown. At times, teacakes, orange juice, lemonade, and iced tea were served to guests who stopped off there. After a brief rest, perhaps in one of the rocking chairs made by L. B. Brown, guests continued on their way.[2]

Lawrence Brown eventually owned a large amount of real estate; meanwhile his business dealings built for him a reputation admired over a wide area. His holdings eventually included over forty properties. In 1912, a Jacksonville newspaper confirmed the fact. "Mr. L. B. Brown is erecting many new houses in the community at this time," it reported. "He is doing a splendid job and is the leading property owner in Bartow among the gentlemen of color." By the time that L.B. Brown died in 1941, his estate had become a substantial one.

At the time of his death, five heirs were still alive: Louvenia, Lorenzo, Clifford, Mary, and Robert. Louvenia lived in Winter Haven and Clifford in Lakeland. Mary, Lorenzo, and Robert lived in the L. B. Brown House. In the late 1940s Robert moved to Jacksonville and later, in the 1960s, he relocated to New York City. Lorenzo died in April of 1959 and Mary died in September of 1966. After Mary died, leaving the house vacant, Louvenia moved in.

Eventually Louvenia's finances and health led to the deterioration of the house. She was a respected school teacher and involved in church activities including attending local and national church conferences. She had no children and later was widowed. In time, her expenses exceeded her income. In her later years, she experienced crippling arthritis and other medical conditions that confined her to a wheelchair.

Not able to keep the home in good repair, she at times required help paying property taxes. Hopeful of putting the beloved property to good use, she deeded it to various friends with the desire that they save it for charitable use, such as for a retirement home. When she died in 1989, the house's decline unfortunately seemed inevitable. As the deterioration continued into the mid-1990s, building code violations caused the historic property to be a candidate for demolition.

Around 1998 Bartow's Neighborhood Improvement Corporation stepped forward. Its officers and members inaugurated efforts to acquire and restore the Brown Home. Other organizations and individuals stepped up as well, and restoration proceeded. Thereafter, the question became what to do with the structure. Should it be a community center, an educational facility, or a museum? A growing consensus emerged as to its role as a historical museum and a tribute to the life and accomplishments of L. B. Brown.

Achieving a Place on the National Register of Historic Places

An effort proceeded in 2000 to secure a listing for the Brown House on the National Register of Historic Places. Respected historical consultant Sidney Johnston offered an excellent characterization and description of the house that remains helpful today. First, he noted descriptive items that had appeared in the DeLand *Florida Agriculturist* on November 14, 1894, and January 30, 1895. The first observed: "All wood houses in this country [i.e., region are built upon block or brick piers, and should be at least two feet above the ground so that the foundation can be easily repaired. That also gives a free circulation under the house. Twenty by thirty feet, with sixteen feet studding is a good size, and there should be sixteen windows, four on each side and ends. There should be no mortising in the frame, but everything nailed together, a regular balloon frame. The frame should be well braced with a square roof. The house should be covered with novelty siding."[3]

The second one added: "A bedroom should never be on the lower floor of a southern house. All the partitions in such a house can be made of ceiling, and should be ceiled overhead, in the chambers to keep out the heat and soot, as most everyone burns pine wood. Porches need not be deep, as six feet gives a very good porch. Such a house ought to be built here for $250, but location as to facilities for obtaining materials would add to or decrease the cost."

Sidney Johnston in center with members of the volunteer group Polk County Wood Turners. Ralph Gineau, President of Wood Turners on the right.

Johnston supplemented that information with specific information on the Brown House and added the benefit of his conclusions. As stated in his report to the US Department of Interior, his summary noted, in part:

> The Lawrence Bernard Brown House is located at 470 Second Avenue [now L. B. Brown Ave. in Bartow. The two-story wood Frame Vernacular residence displays an irregularly massed cross-gable Z-plan, metal crimp panel roof surfacing, corbeled brick

chimneys, and a tiered veranda. Patterned wood shingles and drop siding protect the wood balloon framework, and fenestration is asymmetrical and irregular with double-hung sash windows displaying various shapes and light arrangements. The common character of this well-executed, but traditional wood frame dwelling is obscured by unique nineteenth century picturesque millwork, including barge boards, leaded glass transoms and sidelights, gingerbread, turned posts, spindle work, jigsaw cut balusters, variegated wood shingles and a Palladian window, or a serliana, opening. Derived from Queen Anne stylistic influences, the millwork and window patterns offer an encyclopedia of late nineteenth century detailing. The foundation consists of a combination of brick and tree-trunk piers. It contains approximately fifteen hundred square feet of interior floor space and displays a superior level of craftmanship. The dwelling retains its late-nineteenth-century character and integrity to a high degree. The owner, Neighborhood Improvement Corporation of Bartow, Inc. is currently rehabilitating the resource.[4]

Physical Description
Exterior

By design, the dwelling was constructed so that each elevation displays a prominent cross-gable embellished wood products. This design ensures that the elaborate detailing of the dwelling is visible from any elevation.

The front or west facade is asymmetrical with a cross-gable plan. The front-facing gable is finished with fish scale and square cut wood shingles, and the fascia is trimmed with jigsaw cut barge boards displaying spindles and curvilinear patterns. An attic louver occupies a space where leaded glass was originally installed, and is presently being conserved in preparation for re-installation.

Alterations

The alterations to the building appear to date from the historic period. Tree trunks appear to have served as the original pier foundation system. Many of the trunks along the exterior walls were later replaced, c. 1925, with sand-lime bricks. The southeast corner of the dwelling and interior points of the foundation system are still supported by tree trunks. Built about 1910, a one-story hip-roof extension projects at the southeast corner. The character of the exterior wall fabric indicates that the one-story extension was built after the completion of the original dwelling. Sanborn Company maps confirm that the addition was completed before 1917. The shed-roof porch at the rear elevation was built around 1950.

Architectural Significance

A good example of Frame Vernacular construction, the Brown House displays irregular massing with projecting cross gables. The second-floor, especially, displays the unusual Z-plan of the house. The c. 1910 one-story hip extension on the first floor conveys the erroneous impression that the house was built using a modified L-plan.

A break from the formal symmetry of house design in the early nineteenth century, irregularly massed dwellings were not folk derived, but instead were promoted by architects and builders in plan books, eventually becoming a popular building type in the late nineteenth century. Towns that grew vigorously in the late nineteenth century because of an improved railroad network required substantial numbers of dwellings. Irregularly-massed dwellings, especially those displaying shapes, became a popular house form reflecting the predilections of home owners and builders.

Lawrence Brown, an African-American carpenter who learned his craft during the Reconstruction period, developed the house in the 1890s using design and construction patterns familiar to him.

The Brown house transcends the traditional association of African-Americans relying on Shotgun-style architecture to build their communities. Uncharacteristic in its Z plan and heavily adorned, the house contributes a sense of time, place, and historical development through its ambiance, linkage, and character to the historic built fabric of Bartow.

A watershed moment arrived in the year 2000. The NIC applied for and received listing on the National Register of Historic Places.

African American Heritage Conference and Festival

The next year, the first African American Heritage Conference and Festival was held on its grounds, drawing thousands of visitors. The inspiration for the Conference and Festival came from historian Canter Brown. (Currently retired from Fort Valley State University.) He shared his idea with Clifton Lewis and Mike Denham. (James "Mike" Denham, Ph.D. Professor of History and Director of the Lawton M. Chiles, Jr. Center for Florida History at Florida Southern College.) Once the idea was agreed upon, Canter Brown recruited Larry Rivers (Larry E. Rivers, Ph.D. Distinguished Professor of History Florida A & M University.) to help with the planning and organizing.

These three distinguished historians sent out invitations to scholars throughout the Southeast to participate in this first African American Heritage Conference and Festival. They organized the event as well as presented papers themselves. Under a tent erected in the lot next to the house, scholars shared pertinent and fascinating research discoveries. The public was welcomed. Food vendors and entertainment, much as is true of the Festival today, offered diversions and amenities. With the success of the Festival, the house and property again began to serve as a focal point for the community.

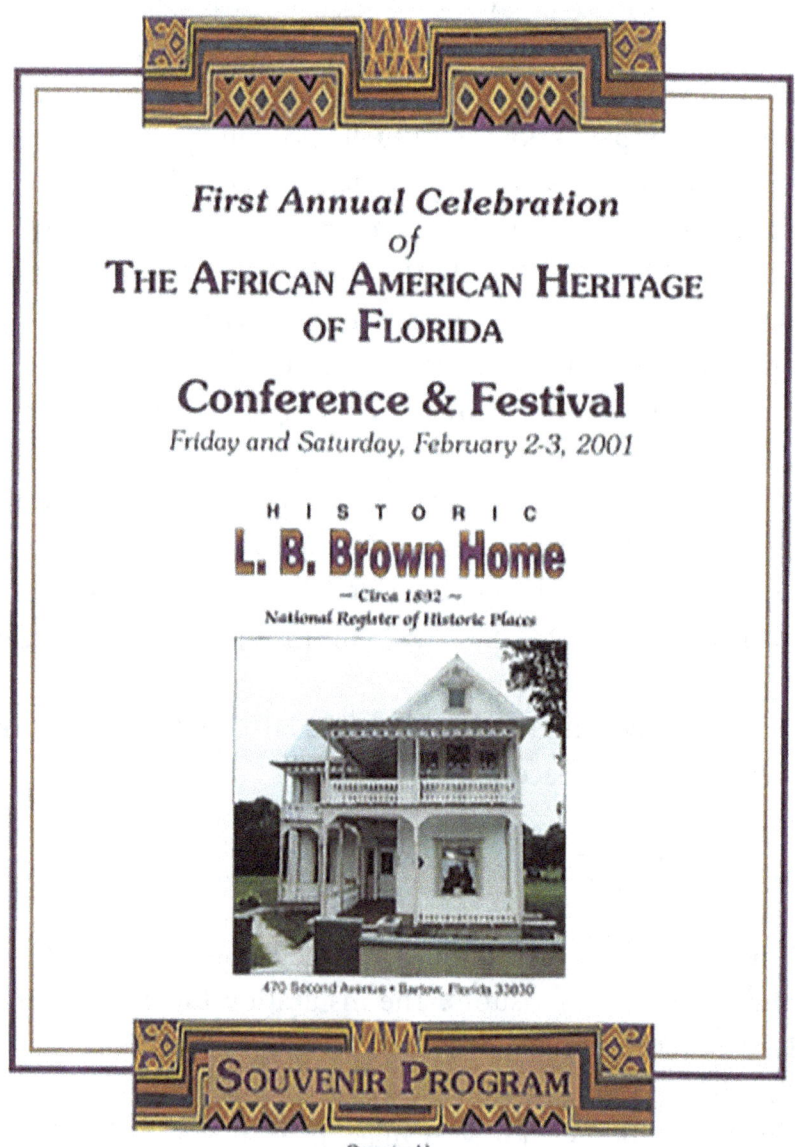

Flyer for First Annual Conference and Festival

First African American Heritage Conference

The First African American Heritage Festival at L. B. Brown House Museum

2nd Infantry Regiment United States Colored Troops teach history to school children

Before restoration side view

THE L. B. BROWN HOUSE/MUSEUM

Before restoration front view

The L.B. Brown House and Museum. Photo by: Courtesy of The L.B. Brown House and Museum

After restoration

The Historic LB Brown House is owned and operated by the Neighborhood Improvement Corporation of Bartow, Inc. Restoration of the main house was completed in 2001. Funds were provided by the Florida Department of State, Division of Historical Resources; the Bartow Community Redevelopment Agency; Community Development Block Grant; and local businesses and residents. The City of Bartow continues to provide significant contributions.

L. B. Brown made these concrete foundation pieces. Notice his initials. An extra foundation piece is on display in the Smithsonian Institute's National Museum of African American History and Culture in Washington D. C.

Plumbing and electricity came about 15 years after the house was built.

The foundation is built on 18 tree logs that remain strong today.

The above sign welcomes visitors to the L. B. Brown House/ Museum. Signs are placed around the house describing the interior and outdoor features. The street running in front of the house was Second Avenue, but has been renamed L. B. Brown Ave.

This stairway is at the main entrance. The decorative wood is typical throughout.

Another example of the detail you will find in every room.

Family photos found in the entryway to the house.

Top row: Annie Bell Brown; L. B. Brown

Second row: Annie Bell Brown; L. B. Brown; Catherine Brown, L. B.'s mother; no photo exists of Peter Brown

Third row: Ben Burnett, Louvenia Thomas, Clifford Brown, Mary Tugerson, Annie Brown, Robert E. L. Brown, and Lorenzo Brown who had been paralyzed by polio

Fourth row: Joseph Tugerson, the son of Mary. LB and Annie's only grandchild

(Note: Spelling of some names varies.)

The Dining Room

The Sitting Room

A portion of the far wall has been cut out to show the original construction work.

A display case located in the sitting room. (On the right in the picture on the previous page.)

The top shelf contains L. B. Brown' personal umbrella and his pocket watch which still works. The second shelf contains L. B.'s book of etiquette—*The Golden Way*, Robert Brown's Pullman Porter cap, Robert's book of Pullman car rules and procedures, his union contract, and L. B.'s Book of Florida Law and Banking Regulations. Lower shelf contains Annie's blue head bonnet.

Another view of the main sitting room

This mirror above the fireplace is in the front sitting room. L. B. Brown silvered the mirror. Notice the decorative wood work around the mirror and fireplace.

The master bedroom, one of four bedrooms upstairs

Some of the intricate detail on the balcony.

Detail above balcony windows

Rental House Built by L. B. Brown

This rental house, built around 1912, was moved to the L. B. Brown Museum site in June 2007 from its original location about a block away on Wabash Ave. It is now a part of the L. B. Brown Museum complex. The house has three bedrooms, hallway, kitchen, living room, and dining room. It is estimated that Brown built over 50 similar houses in the East Bartow area. This house is currently used for meetings and for storing some of the historic artifacts of L. B. Brown and others.

Rental house built by L. B. Brown

CHAPTER 4

The Neighborhood Improvement Corporation Rescues the Brown House/Museum

Making a Difference: A Few Citizens with a Dream

Unaware of the historic twists and turns their efforts would take, a group of six concerned citizens of Bartow gathered at the urging of Clifton Lewis in November 1996. Their aim was to discuss improvement of their neighborhood. Word of this ambitious group's plans spread quickly through the city's African American community. As a result, its ranks swelled to over forty within a few months.

Beginnings

NIC founder and longtime leader Clifton Lewis later detailed the organization's early days and the people who proved instrumental to its eventual success:

> Today, West Bartow is a growing and peaceful neighborhood. Although this historic area still shows the wear and tear of over 150 years of existence, new homes are being built to accommodate new families. The crime rate of all types are relatively low, and longtime residents share bits of family and neighborhood history in a spirit of pride.
>
> But West Bartow was not always this way. At the end of the 1990s, a group of residents came together to reverse the decline of housing and to address the high crime rate.
>
> In 1996, to be exact, a small group of residents came together to address those concerns. The participants initially called themselves "The West Side Improvement Committee" because the original concern was aimed at West Bartow. Notwithstanding the geographical focus on West Bartow, it is interesting to note that a number of those

responding lived on the East Side of Bartow as well as in the unincorporated suburban village of Gordonville.

An early NIC meeting

Among those who answered the initial call of organizer Clifton P. Lewis were the Reverend Earl Brown Williams, Willie Myrick, Jr., Mabel Leonard, Ben Williams, Gwen Strong, Jimmie Burt, Myrtice Nico, and Willie Bush.

The first meeting was held at 11:00 a.m. on a Monday in November 1996. The informal gathering was held at the First Providence Missionary Baptist Church, located at 1030 West King Street. Following a brief discussion of their concerns, everyone agreed that something had to be done.

Reverend Williams offered the support of First Providence Missionary Baptist Church. He offered the use of church facilities for future meetings without charge. All subsequent meetings over the next few years were hosted by the First Providence MB Church.

Receiving such robust backing from the Pastor of that historic old church served as a symbolic "good housekeeping stamp of approval." This endorsement inspired other residents and business leaders to join the effort. Adding clout to his initial endorsement, Reverend Williams used his Sunday sermons to urge support for the group. This was the first major acceptance of the effort and pretty much guaranteed its success.

Operating under the name West Bartow Improvement Committee, the group held several more meetings during the months of November and December. Members agreed that in order to make meaningful improvements, the support of Bartow city administration was essential. Toward that end, an invitation was extended to the city manager, Joseph DeLegge, who agreed to meet with the group; that meeting was held in early January 1997.

Prior to the start of that January meeting, members toured the neighborhood in a van made available by Reverend Williams. As the van moved slowly along each street in the neighborhood, seniors in the group provided historical commentary for the benefit of City Manager Delegge. After the tour, DeLegge stated that in his many years living in Bartow he had been unaware of the history of West Bartow, and he appreciated learning its rich history.

During the meeting, the city manager offered his full support and said that he would direct department heads to provide all assistance possible. True to his word, he attended subsequent Monday morning meetings along with heads of various city departments. Acting at the city manager's direction, the Parks and Recreation Manager assigned a supervisor to attend our weekly meetings and report progress.

In addition to Reverend Williams and DeLegge, the group reached out to Mrs. Mayme (Burden) Clark who served as Executive Director of the Bartow Chamber of Commerce. Mrs. Clark pledged the full support of the Chamber. She also reached out to Mr. George Harris, President of the Citrus and Chemical Bank and secured his support for the group.

Mr. Harris was one of the most influential movers and shakers in the Polk County business community, and, in that capacity, he used his influence to let it be known among his peers that he stood behind this effort. To assist the business model of this emerging organization, Mr. Harris assigned several bank executives from C & C Bank to attend the meetings and offer their business perspective.

The Reverend Jim Hatch, pastor of the First Presbyterian Church of Bartow, became a key person in the development of the Neighborhood Improvement Corporation. Pastor Hatch offered his personal support and encouraged members of his congregation to get involved. Among First Presbyterian members who made significant contributions were Albert Reese and Chuck Bentley. Both of these gentlemen agreed to serve as charter members of the board of directors after it was decided to formally incorporate the informal "West Bartow Improvement Committee."

Chuck Bentley, who served as an attorney with the Holland and Knight Law Firm, recruited Sandy Sheets, another Holland and Knight attorney, to help edit the bylaws. George Harris offered to pay the incorporation fee, approximately two hundred dollars. Clifton Lewis, the newly elected founding president, thanked Mr. Harris for his generosity, but instead challenged the members to demonstrate their commitment by reaching into their pockets to raise the money. That spontaneous collection raised nearly four hundred dollars, with Jeff Bagwell, president of the Lakeland based Keystone Challenge Fund contributing two hundred dollars. The willingness of the members to pay their own way sent a clear signal that the group was serious. Attorneys Bentley and Sheets proceeded to apply for incorporation. On April 1, 1997, the group became incorporated as The Neighborhood Improvement Corporation of Bartow, Inc. (NIC).

Albert Reese, due to his involvement in affordable housing, chaired the housing committee. Geraldine Watson and Jeffery Hoch organized a neighborhood cleanup. The cleanup was held in March 1998 with nearly three hundred persons from all parts of Bartow participating. It was quite a sight to see men, women, and children of all ages and races picking up paper, climbing trees to trim branches, and hauling huge trash bags. Among the hardest workers were Tom Mathews, the Executive Director of Bartow Memorial Hospital; Bartow City Manager Joe DeLegge and other city employees; and the pastor of First Providence, E. B. Williams, and the pastor of First Presbyterian, Jim Hatch along with members from their churches.

First NIC Mission Statement

Mission

It is the Mission of the Neighborhood Improvement Corporation of Bartow, Inc. to nurture a safe, healthy, dynamic and beautiful environment in which the essence, the energy and the substance of community will flourish in the city of Bartow, Florida. We shall be the catalyst for unification and positive change in the neighborhoods of Bartow by organizing and empowering them to grow, to build, and to sustain themselves and the City. We are committed to bridging every gap in the achievement of educational and economic success; to eliminating every racial divide; and to opening every door behind which opportunity stands. We entrust our mind, our hearts and our souls to the promise of the future.

Where there is no vision, the people perish. (Proverbs 29:18) became their motto.

> **NIC Charter members:**
>
> | | |
> |---|---|
> | Mabel Leonard | Jeffery Hoch |
> | Gloria McCoy | Tom Mathews |
> | Myrtice Nico | Geraldine O. Watson |
> | Mollie Marion | Roland Stephens |
> | Alvin B. Smith | Ben Williams |
> | Mary Bryant | Chuck Bentley |
> | Albert Reese | |
>
> Clifton P. Lewis - Founding President

Over the next several months, the decision was made to focus their efforts on the following areas:

1. Development of a Master Plan for the creation of a model neighborhood.
2. Improve street lighting (replace bulbs, add additional lights).
3. Polk Street uplift (new street lamps and poles, landscaping with sprinklers, and sidewalks).
4. Improve drainage.
5. Crime prevention—eliminate drug traffic.
6. Vigorous code enforcement (dilapidated structures, abandoned cars, number of residents per unit, etc.).

The NIC members knew that, in order to properly address these concerns, money would be needed. Very little infrastructure improvement had been accomplished in the area since its settlement nearly 150 years earlier. The neighborhood required more paved streets, proper sidewalks, an expanded sewage system, storm water management, street lighting, regular trash pickup, and effective law enforcement.

City Manager DeLegge acknowledged the existence of these conditions and pledged to work with the NIC to address them. DeLegge made the group aware of an annual appropriation of Federal funds known as the Community Development Block Grant (CDBG) and suggested that these funds might be channeled to West Bartow.

To everyone's surprise, West Bartow was ineligible to receive this grant because it was not considered to be a low-income community. Research by Doug Leonard of the Central Florida Regional Planning Council (CFRPC) revealed that when census tracts were drawn West Bartow had been grouped with contiguous higher income neighborhoods. This caused the average income to rank above the poverty guidelines.

To correct this situation, a door-to-door census count needed to be completed detailing family size, income, job status and ages of each member of the household. CFRPC staff developed a questionnaire and led the canvass. NIC members accompanied CFRPC staff to help residents feel more comfortable answering sensitive questions asked by strangers.

This effort resulted in West Bartow becoming eligible to receive CDBG funds. It also helped Bartow by increasing the amount of grant funds available to the city.

History Comes Into Focus

The NIC initially planned to tear down abandoned and dilapidated buildings. West Bartow's African-American community, excited about the effort to clean up the neighborhood and make it safer, moved ahead eagerly. Activists soon found, however, that some residents were reluctant to accept changes so quickly. The older residents recognized that many of the dilapidated buildings represented history that ought to be preserved. It would be good, the elders suggested, to capture the history of the buildings before tearing them down. They considered West Bartow to be unique. They understood the importance of preserving the special character and identity of the area.

Cleaning up West Bartow

In response to those concerns, Lewis reached out to historians Canter Brown, Jr. and James M. "Mike" Denham, both of whom enjoyed longstanding ties with Polk County. They agreed to consult without charge and went on to play major roles in bringing the importance of community history into the NIC effort. Their leadership was noted in Clifton Lewis's call for historical information entitled "The Forgotten Legacy—Recapturing the Missing Pieces: A History Project of African Americans In Bartow 1849-1997." In his request the NIC leader quoted from Dr. Brown's book *African Americans on the Tampa Bay Frontier*:

> African Americans had played an essential and continuing role in the settlement and development of the southwest Florida frontier of the 1800s…Tragically, by the early decades of this century most of their story had been shoved aside, hidden behind the veil of the past…Seldom did they even mention the passing of [black individuals worthy of admiration and respect…The loss has touched all Americans."

Lewis added: "But fortunately things are changing. Thanks to a more enlightened society and historians such as Canter Brown, Jr. and Mike Denham—men of immense professional integrity—we have the unprecedented opportunity to not only participate in the research of our history but to lead the effort to reconstruct it."

He ends with another quote from Canter Brown: "Our ancestors lived, contributed and died…and today they remain buried. But if we bring them back by writing about them in a book, they will come alive again—and this time they will never die."

To accomplish the goal, a historical committee coalesced. The work proved challenging, but—as the history emerged—it became obvious that West Bartow could boast far more positives than negatives. Gratefully, many of the older residents spoke willingly of the past, both the good and the bad. Sadly, their discussions about past race relations sometimes proved painful. The fact remains that black persons often describe race relations in negative terms.

Over a period of several years, the idea developed to rebuild a community rooted in a foundation of lessons, accomplishments, and role models that the past can provide to those living today. As Lewis insisted, "Our history can empower our present."

History: Lessons and Role Models for Today

Until recently, histories of Florida and its various regions tragically ignored or minimized the accomplishments of African Americans. Compounding this problem, the state's population has largely been born elsewhere. This has resulted unfortunately in a relative lack of interest in exploring Florida's past.

As the NIC delved into its community's history, members uncovered fascinating detail that had been long-forgotten. For example, black persons' contributions to industries such as brick making and raising cattle surfaced. They learned, too, that black men actually prospected for phosphate as well as worked in the mines, that fruit packing provided a source of employment, and that skilled craftsmen lived in the area. They discovered active social lives had existed with social clubs, night clubs, soda fountains, movie houses, lodges, and activities that offered many forms of entertainment.

Another side of life came to view, as well. Oldtimers discussed seldom-revealed details about gambling, describing the game of bolita including how it was played and sometimes fixed. Avoiding police detection and maintaining respectability often demanded creativity. Still, bolita at one time had offered a source of income during hard times to numerous families.

Not all the discoveries involved African Americans. The names of prominent white businessmen who served as financial backers to the bolita runners were revealed, subject to a promise of confidentiality even though the men had long since died. In a related financial vein, black men could not obtain loans through normal banking channels. Loan sharks had stepped into the vacuum to offer loans at exorbitant interest rates, some as high as 100 percent.

Learning about community institutions, the early churches, and schools opened to NIC members an amazing new view of West Bartow history. For example: the present-day First Providence Missionary Baptist Church most likely originated around 1856. At that time members of Polk County's enslaved pioneers began worshipping in open fields near Bear Creek in West Bartow. Years later, a church building rose. First Providence possibly stands as the oldest black church and the oldest continuing black institution of any kind in Polk County as well as in much of Central and South Florida.

Similarly, records suggest that the first public school for black children in the county opened its doors locally in the mid-1880s. Eventually known as the Brittsville School, the two-story wooden building served the West Bartow community until demolished in the 1940s when the school merged with Union Academy.

Although West Bartow recently stood as a self-contained, racially segregated community with its own institutions and social order, its existence reached back well over a century. It carried from the late 1880s the name Brittsville in honor of white developer William F. Britt, who built the first planned subdivision in this black area. African-American residents, though, preferred to call it "Over the Branch" because one needed to cross over McKinney Creek to get to other parts of town.

As the NIC's research progressed, Canter Brown and Mike Denham encouraged members to further explore early black pioneers and their contributions to Bartow's development. Among these pioneers were Andy Moore who, after being freed, became a successful farmer; Elizabeth Moore (1867-1905), daughter of Andy Moore and Tanner Reid Moore who married Thomas Waldon and homesteaded 160 acres in Homeland and later the Moore homestead in West Bartow; former slave Stepney Dixon who, in 1867, accepted an appointment as one of three county voter registrars, making him the first black person to serve in a county office in Polk County; Prince Johnson, who became the first black person to run for county office (he ran for constable, but was not successful) and later gained respect as a prosperous farmer and tradesman; and many more.

The L. B. Brown House/Museum

Buttressed by the product of its research effort, the NIC in 1997 expanded its scope beyond West Bartow. Specifically, it began the process of acquiring and preserving the old abandoned Brown House.

Vendarae Lewis, Juanita Warner, Dr. Canter Brown, the Polk County Historical Association's Freddie Wright, Dr. Mike Denham and Alvin Smith discuss the restoration project.

In that effort, NIC research paid off impressively. Members used the history they had recovered as a way of salvaging the Brown House, utilizing its legacy to enhance the surrounding community. They not only took on the Brown House restoration project to preserve an important historical structure but also to illustrate what could be done to improve an area if the community worked together.

From these beginnings, the project to restore the house received broad support. Prominent politicians such as John Laurent and Adam Putnam pledged their backing. City Manager DeLegge threw the weight of the city's resources behind the effort. The Polk County Historical Association printed articles about the house and African American history in its quarterly publication, and President Freddie Wright urged her members to get involved. The restoration effort brought people of all races and ethnic backgrounds together for this common vision. Understandably, many residents expressed interest as they knew the Brown family and respected its members as successful community entrepreneurs and examples of personal accomplishment.

The family's name once more became attached to the site. For years in the late twentieth century the old house had been called "Mrs. Thomas' house" because Louvenia Brown Thomas, daughter of Lawrence and Annie Brown, was the last person to have lived there. Her memory continued to be honored by the community, but her home once again went by the name with which she was born.

The lessons learned as a result of the outstanding counsel provided by the two scholars, Canter Brown and Mike Denham, turned out to be of immense benefit in helping to recognize the important historical value of the old house and the legacy of its builder, Lawrence Brown. During one of his visits to Bartow, Lawrence and Annie's youngest child Robert commented to Clifton Lewis after restoration had begun, "When my father built this house…" Stunned, Lewis asked Robert to repeat what he had just said. "Oh, yes, my dad built this house." Until that time, Lewis had thought that the NIC simply was restoring an old house of historical value. But this bit of information raised its intrinsic and historical value immensely. Crediting Brown and Denham for their input, Lewis has acknowledged that he immediately understood the importance of the revelation.

Research conducted following that day's sudden revelation about the builder has confirmed that Lawrence Brown, indeed, did build the house.

As a volunteer-staffed nonprofit organization, the NIC often relied upon professionals willing to work pro bono. Local attorney John Murphy, for one, performed legal research to clear up the very convoluted deed. When he began the work, it was unclear how many people possessed or asserted an ownership interest in the house, valid or not. Some claims went back decades, some came from tax assessments sold by the county. The most significant deed holder was Loraine Jones, a friend of Louvenia Thomas who had received the property as a donation. Mrs. Jones died not long after receiving the deed, thus negotiations had to be opened with her heirs.

Happily, the last living Brown heir, Robert E. L. Brown, traveled from his home in New York City to offer monetary and moral support for the effort. While in Bartow, he deeded several pieces of property around the house to the NIC. The organization finally purchased the home and property from the last deedholder for $20,000 in 1999.

At that point, restoration could begin. The Florida Bureau of Historical Resources contributed a grant of $14,500 and the Bartow Community Redevelopment Agency gave another $10,000. The NIC appealed to community pride and the spirit of volunteerism. Individual monetary assistance came in, city workers removed trash and yard debris, and the Florida State Division of Historical Preservation furnished additional funding. As recounted by Clifton Lewis, the Polk County Woodturners and the Winter Haven Woodcrafters donated their labor for restoring the distinctive "gingerbread" detailing.

Other repairs included stabilizing the foundation, treatment for termites, painting, and repair of windows, doors, and roof. A $138,000 grant from the Bureau of Historical Resources was used for architectural designs and structural repairs. The NIC's initial estimate of $30,000 for restoration grew to $250,000.

The effort to acquire and restore the L. B. Brown House began in 1997 and successfully ended in 2002. The home serves as a popular tourist attraction where visitors can learn about local African American history, and it provides a forum for students to explore their community's history. Since its restoration, the L. B. Brown House has become a source of pride to residents of Bartow, Polk County, and the State of Florida.

Volunteers cleaning West Bartow. The red shirts signify volunteers from Columbia Bartow Memorial Hospital.

Clifton Lewis leading an organizational meeting

Jeff Hoch, Executive Vice-President of Citrus and Chemical Bank at an organizational meeting.

Sandy Sheets, attorney with Holland and Knight Law Firm, discussing the development of the by-laws and the 501c3 application.

THE NEIGHBORHOOD IMPROVEMENT CORPORATION RESCUES THE BROWN HOUSE/MUSEUM

March 3, 1997 preparing for tour of West Bartow. From left: Jim Hatch, pastor First Presbyterian Church; Rev. Earl B. Williams, pastor First Providence Church; Chuck Bentley, attorney and partner at Holland and Knight Law Firm; Clifton Lewis.

Joe DeLegge (blue jacket) City Manager in 1997 Westside Planning Committee meeting—the precursor to the Neighborhood Improvement Corporation of Bartow, Inc.

NIC retreat July 12, 1997 with Doug Leonard, Central Florida Regional Planning Council Executive Director, leading a strategic planning session.

Early NIC board members from top left: Chuck Warren, author, Annie Keith, Clifton Lewis, Jeff Hoch, Alvin Smith, Myrtic Nicko, Roland Stephens, unknown, Charley McNeil. Seated: Juanita Warner, Mary Bryant, Molly Marion, Gloria McCoy, unknown.

THE NEIGHBORHOOD IMPROVEMENT CORPORATION RESCUES THE BROWN HOUSE/MUSEUM

Dr. Canter Brown, Jr. talking with Dr. Larry E. Rivers at the L. B. Brown House/Museum

Polk County Wood Turners who reproduced the Gingerbread Trim. From left: Ralph Gineau, President of Turners; Cliff Sessons; Clifton Lewis; and unknown member of Wood Turners.

Chapter 5

A Search for Truth

The search for truth about L. B. Brown already has led us down Florida's peninsula in the Reconstruction and post-Reconstruction eras and well into the Twentieth Century at Bartow. There he made a home, pursued a skilled profession, established a family, and helped to build a community. But we still yearn to better understand the man himself. Glimmers of insight have appeared along the way, but a fuller understanding has proven elusive.

Fortunately, a solution to the problem has come to hand. L. B. Brown recorded many of his thoughts and details of his struggles with life's questions in the pages of one of his favorite books—*The Golden Way to the Highest Attainments.* This work informed his thinking, caused him to reflect on meaning and purpose, and provided him guidance in his behavior. He noted his thoughts in its margins, folded over the corners of pages of importance, underlined paragraphs that called out to him, and placed brackets around passages of great meaning to him. It counseled him on how to live. By chance, *The Golden Way* was found in Brown's home inside a sealed fireplace along with two canisters of old phonograph records likely placed there by his oldest daughter Louvenia who was the last person to live in the home. All illustrations in this chapter are from *The Golden Way*.

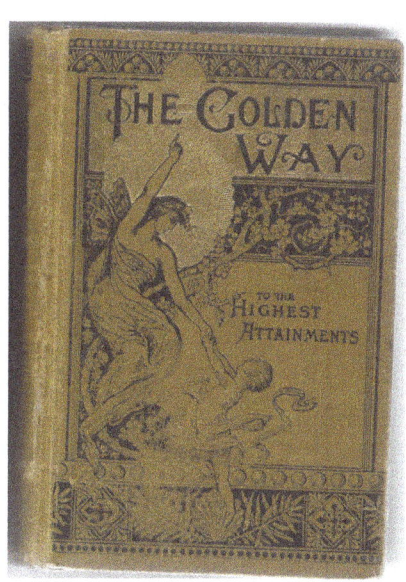

The Golden Way counseled L. B. Brown on how to live

The title page of Brown's copy of *The Golden Way,* published at Chicago in 1889 (about the time he began to call Bartow home), appeared as follows:

111

OUR THRONES AND CROWNS; OR,

THE Golden Way

TO THE

HIGHEST ATTAINMENTS.

A Complete Encyclopædia of Life.

PHYSICAL LIFE, INTELLECTUAL LIFE, BUSINESS LIFE, HOME LIFE, SOCIAL LIFE, MORAL LIFE, RELIGIOUS LIFE, DAILY LIFE, THE DISCIPLINE OF LIFE.

AND THE BEST PREPARATION FOR

The Life Beyond,

BY

REV. J. H. POTTS, D.D.

Author of "The Golden Dawn, or Light on the Great Future, &c."

Embellished with Numerous Full Page Illuminated Plates and Beautiful Engravings.

INTERNATIONAL PUBLISHING CO.,
Chicago, Ill; Philadelphia, Pa.

Title page for The Golden Way

A later page is inscribed with Brown's signature and the date April 18, 1890.

* * *

Neighborhood Improvement Corporation leader Clifton Lewis preserved his record of Brown's notations in *The Golden Way*. Spelling and grammar appear sometimes in a corrected form.

Table of Contents

Even *The Golden Way's* Table of Contents afforded clues to Brown's interests. He highlighted them by bracketing the phrases: "The Secrets of Success," "Home Life," "What is Love," "Choice of Companion," "What a Gentleman is," "Hints to Husbands—Avoid Contradicting," "Hints to Wives—Attend to Small Matters," "Peace at Home," "A Perfect Home," "My Own Fireside," "Social Life," "Will-Power—Firmness of Will and What Will Can Do," "Defamation of Bad Character," and "Christianity and Morality."

* * *

On Women

A loose blank page contained these hand-written notes:

1) In China, where men will marry women and cripple their feet: it is said what women have lost in their feet they've added to their tongue.
2) A woman's tongue is a sword and she'll not let it rust.

* * *

Home Life/Love and Sympathy

Beside the following poem, Brown entered a single word: "Help."

Sympathy
Our hearts, my love, were doomed to be
The genuine twins of sympathy;
They live with one sensation;

In joy or grief, but most in love,
Our heart-strings musically move,
And thrill with like vibration.

How often have I heard thee say,
Thy vital pulse shall cease to play
When mine no more is moving!
Since, now, to feel a joy alone
Were worse to thee than feeling none:
Such sympathy in loving!

"DELIBERATION IS WISDOM."

* * *

James Berry Bensel's poem "Sympathy" follows. As used here, the word includes compassion and empathy. Brown recorded the word "me" next to the poem along with the date "8-1-97."

In sorrow once there came to me
Two friends to proffer sympathy.
One pressed warm dewy lips on mine,
And quoted from the word divine:
Wiped the hot tear-drops from my eye
And gave my sore heart sigh for sigh:
Told me of pain he had outgrown—
Pain that was equal to my own,
And left me with a tender touch
That should have comforted me much.
But still my sorrow was no less
For all his loving graciousness.

The other only pressed my hand;
Within his eyes the tears did stand.
He said no word, but laid a rare
Bunch of sweet flowers beside my chair;
And closely held my hand the while
He cheered my sad gloom with his smile.
And ere he went he sang a song
That I had known and loved for long.
And then he clasped my hand again
With the same look that shares a pain.
And when he went I laid my head
Down, and was glad and comforted.

What was the difference, can you tell?
I loved my friends, alike and well;
I loved them both alike, and yet
The one's warm kiss I could forget,
The other's hand-clasp I could feel
For hours through all my being steal.
Each shared my sorrow, yet to me
One brought but love, one sympathy.

* * *

The Choice of a Companion

Brown drew a hand to mark the following paragraph. (His son Robert recalled that his father's drawing of a pointing hand signified the importance of that object.)

Consider what a wife ought to be. Be not influenced alone by personal attractions. Let not the money question settle your choice. Money and lands are good, but utterly out of place when weighed in the balance against intellectual and moral endowments.

*"Manhood matured with wisdom's Fruit
Succeeds as Autumn Follows Summer's prime"*

Further down on the same page Brown underlined:

Inquire diligently of her disposition, and how her parents have been inclined in their youth.

The Wedding/The Marriage State

The next page advises about the choice of a companion. Brown remarked: "This should be very carefully read before marrying."

He also heavily marked the sections on "**The Wedding**" and "**The Marriage State.**"

In the section on married life, he entered the date January 29, 1917, and bracketed the information there on a bridegroom.

Interestingly, even though he was in his third marriage and had been married for eight years, courtship and marriage continued to interest him.

* * *

*"The days of infancy are all a dream
How Fair, but oh! How short they seem.
'Tis Life's sweet opening Spring."*

Physical Habits

Brown highlighted the following passages regarding physical habits:

There is an intellectual and moral side to the question of habits; but the physical tendency of them is marked and powerful. This is shown by the fact that animals form habits to which they are completely subject. In time of battle, old worn-out war-horses have been known to form in squadrons of their own accord, and charge upon other horses, or mules or fences, and keep up the practice until the commanding and musketry ceased. In the fire-department of great cities, horses may be found with habits which make them as convenient and useful as if they could be reasoned with.

Physical Habits Related to Smoking

Business men sometimes express themselves in the most practical sort of way respecting the use of tobacco. A young merchant of sixteen was observed to enter a mechanics office and apply for a situation to learn the trade.
I might give you a place, but you carry a very bad recommendation in your mouth," said the gentleman.

* * *

Living a Good Life

The introduction, entitled "The Life That Now Is," carried the following bracketed words:

The records of poverty and crime tell us the wicked are the unfortunate. Those who have yielded to the lower nature are in troubles manifold and in exact ratio to such yielding. Those on the other hand who live for the higher nature and who serve God, have at their doors the best rewards and success of this life. Virtue, integrity and holiness at last win the race against their opposites. (Edge of page folded.)

* * *

What Educator Should Be

Brown turned back the corner of a page to note the section entitled, "Reading as a Means of Improvement."

The mind, relaxing into needful sport,
Should turn to writers of an abler sort,
Whose wit, well managed, and whose classic style,
Gives truth a luster, and make wisdom smile.

Would you know what to read? Study your own defects. Adapt your efforts at acquirement not only to what best suits your taste, but to what you most need in order to be most useful. It is wholesome and bracing for the mind to have its faculties kept on the stretch.

* * *

Social/ Woman

"I Wonder"

Brown heavily marked a paragraph dealing with the mistreatment of women through the years. On page 236, he circled the following:

"The cultured woman is the charm of society. Her words, her ways, her deeds, her smiles, enliven the social circle and make permanent its attractions. Her work and influence are a blessing anywhere. They are only beginning to develop, but are destined to constitute the chief surprises among utilitarian accomplishments in the coming years."

"Woman, in her own way, is a creature of might."

He dated August 1, 1897, in this same section and bracketed the following poem:

"Nor steel nor fire itself hath power,
Like woman in her conquering hour.
Be thou but fair—mankind adore thee!
Smile—and a world is weak before thee!"

On January 20, 1898, L. B. Brown also bracketed a passage on the disagreeable woman—the woman who is loud and overbearing and "puffed up with conceit and selfishness…."

He inserted "1907" in the margin next to the following:

The past has disclosed the whole secret of women's conquering power. Fair in her virtue smiling in her goodness, she wields an influence which mailed warrior never could. Her strength is in her graces, her weapon is love; and her power is resistless when these are combined with modest merit, and dictated by conscious duty.

* * *

The Reality of Christian Experience

Brown relied on his Christian faith to find answers to questions about life and society. He questioned how to live a quality life and searched for answers through passages such as the following.

He underlined the following sentence:

The desire of self-justification," said he [Martin Luther, "is the cause of all the distresses of the heart. But he who receives Jesus Christ as a savior, enjoys peace; and not only peace, but purity of heart."

"The Book That Meets All Wants"

The Bible and Its Study

Brown bracketed a paragraph that stated, in part:

It is not needful that we shake in alarm at infidel attacks upon the Bible. It has always been so, and perhaps always will be.

He marked the sentence:

To enjoy the Bible, first of all, get a copy that is well-printed, nicely bound, and of convenient size.

He underlined:

Study your Bible, with all the helps at command, but if you have not a dictionary or a commentary, yet study it thoroughly.

* * *

The Discipline of Life

He bracketed the following paragraph on parenting:

"If we are not truthful," he (J. B. Walker) therefore observes "we shall sow the seeds of infidelity, which, long after we are gone, shall spring from our coffined clay and bear fruit unto death. Children may be too strictly reared, but never too deeply impressed with the value of truth. Let us as parents be careful what we promise and threaten; but when we have deliberately spoken however costly, however painful, let us fulfill."

"Teach Children to Help Themselves"

* * *

The Discipline of Life/Affliction and Its Benefits

Brown bracketed a thought by Rev. Dr. Theodore L. Cuyler:

Our heavenly Father often lays heavy burdens upon us, which he could easily spare us as far as his power is concerned; but these loads are required to give us spiritual sinew.

He continued to extensively bracket throughout this section indicating his interest in discipline and understanding the meaning of a burdensome life.

* * *

The Discipline of Life/Nuggets by the Way

Brown marked the following paragraph:

Be Right.—A man must not only desire to be right—he must be right. You may say, "I wish to send this ball so as to kill the lion crouching yonder, ready to spring upon me. My wishes are all right, and I hope Providence will direct the ball." Providence won't. You must do it; and if you do not, you are a dead man.

In this same section he dated a passage "1-4-1900."

A High Aim.—If you want to attain to a high type of Christian character, adjust your life and labors clearly, conscientiously, and earnestly after a high ideal. Water rises no higher than its fountain head. Your religious life will never jump up unexpectedly above the average of your motives, aims, aspirations and plans….Be energetic, resolute, determined. Win heaven if you win nothing else….

Two pages afterward, he wrote the same date and marked the following passage:

Exactly Right.—No physician ever weighed out medicine to his patients with half so much exactness and care as God weighs out to us every trial; not one grain too much does He ever permit to be put in the scale.

Chapter 6

A Living Legacy

The Bartow community celebrates and honors L. B. Brown by preserving and holding in high regard the home that he built, evoking his life through events that reflect his successes, and bestowing his name on awards and in places in a manner that helps to keep his example before us. A model of success to all, he came from humble beginnings at a time when education was not easily available to black people. Eventually, he achieved distinction as a successful entrepreneur during a turbulent and dangerous era for people of his race in general and black men in particular.

Brown's contribution of building homes, a remarkable feat in itself, highlights his legacy. He provided housing for families moving to Bartow who were following employment opportunities, many of them tied directly or indirectly to railroads and the mining of phosphate. His efforts elevated the living standard of these freed men and women. At Bartow, courtesy of L. B. Brown's efforts, they enjoyed access to decent housing.

Brown's accomplishments, though, did not all involve wood and nails. His interest in the town—helping to grow a church community and developing educational opportunities for black children—stand out as stellar achievements. He excelled as a role model to others through his generosity and desire to lead a good life. He demonstrated that no matter one's humble beginnings, there lies within each individual the resources to make a contribution. His life provided an example that lifts all who were or are touched by it.

The L. B. Brown House Museum

A visit to the L. B. Brown House Museum takes one on a journey back in time to the late Nineteenth Century. The nine-room, 1,700 square-foot Victorian house is impressive in itself, becoming more so with an understanding that it was built by a man born into slavery who overcame difficult racial barriers with courage, determination, and a will to succeed. The house stands as a testament to resilience and strength.

The Brown House, honored by its presence on the National Register of Historic Places, seemingly exists as the only house in Central Florida built by a person born into slavery that remains standing. Visitors are welcome to walk the grounds to admire its architecture. Inside tours also available. Check the website at www.lbbrown.com for information on scheduling a tour.

L. B. Brown's Home in Bartow, Florida

L. B. Brown Heritage Festival

Beginning in 2000, the Neighborhood Improvement Corporation of Bartow, Inc. has held a three-day L. B. Brown Festival on the grounds of the L. B. Brown House Museum. Every February, the festival has provided the public with educational programs, entertainment, and recognition of citizens who have made outstanding contributions. The following activities generally are included in Festival events:

- L B Brown Youth Leadership Awards—Each year, a number of local middle and high schools select one student to receive this award. The recipient is not restricted by race or gender. During the awards ceremony, an administrator from the student's school shares the student's accomplishments followed by the student's narration of his or her future plans. Each student receives a letter of congratulations and a medallion. Several of the students have used their letter when applying for college admission. The awards ceremony, a powerful affirmation of today's youth, offers a moving experience for participants and attendees.

Program for Youth Leadership Awards

- History lectures and audience discussion: Each year an educational program is presented to enlighten the public regarding the events of L. B. Brown's era. For example, in 2012, Sergeant Jarvis Rosier of the United States Colored Troops presented a lecture on the topic "Slavery to Freedom: African Americans During the Civil War Era."

- Recognition of small business entrepreneurs who, in the spirit of L. B. Brown, are making a significant contribution to the community.

- Living history—demonstrations depicting how people lived in the second half of the 1800s.

- Special groups such as United States Colored Troops reenactors and Black Seminoles explain and exhibit their unique history.

- Local talent entertains with performances including dancing, singing, and poetry.

12th Annual L. B. Brown Heritage Festival
Historic L. B. Brown House Museum c. 1892

SATURDAY, FEBRUARY 11, 2012

MORNING

Lecture and Audience Discussion — 10:30 a.m. – 12:00 Noon
Slavery to Freedom: "African Americans During the Civil War Era"
Sergeant Jarvis Rosier
2nd Inf. Reg., United States Colored Troops • Tallahassee, Florida

AFTERNOON — 1:00 p.m. – 6:00 p.m.

Business Award presentation to Ms. Shayanne Jones – Especially 4-U Restaurant

DJ & Live Band — 1:00 p.m. – 6:00 p.m.
Historical Performance ❈ Crystal World of Dance ❈ Step Team Competition ❈ Hair / Fashion Show ❈ The Gift – Performer ❈ Theology – Performer ❈ Poetry

DAILY — 8:30 a.m. – 6:00 p.m.

- ❖ Tours of Historic L. B. Brown House
  Friday ❈ Saturday ❈ Sunday

- ❖ Back-In-the-Day Living History Demonstrations
  Margaret Smart & Residents for Community Improvement, Inc.
  Gloria Washington, President ❈ Marjorie Patterson ❈ Emma Hymes ❈ Johnnie McNair ❈ Eunice Jennings

- ❖ Mr. Ralph Smith - Black Seminole Indians
  Friday and Saturday

- ❖ Sgt. James Rosier – Civil War Era
  United States Colored Troops
  Friday and Saturday

Admission is free. Vendors will be available all day throughout the weekend. The Black Seminole Indians and the Civil War Era United States Colored Troops (USCT) will be available for photos and to answer questions on Friday and Saturday.

Sponsored by the Neighborhood Improvement Corporation of Bartow, Inc. ❈ City of Bartow ❈ Bartow Community Redevelopment Agency ❈ Chamber of Commerce ❈ Community Southern Bank ❈ Friends of the Bartow Public Library ❈ Attorney Larry D. Hardaway ❈ Leo E. Longworth – State Farm Insurance ❈ Mayme Clark ❈ J. J. Corbett ❈ St. James A. M. E. Church ❈ First Providence M. B. Church ❈ Gause Funeral Home ❈ WSIR Family Radio (1490 AM) ❈ Madrid Engineering Group ❈ Mr. & Mrs. Dudley Putnam

L. B. Brown House Museum c.1892 ❈ 470 L. B. Brown Avenue ❈ Bartow, Florida 33830 ❈ www.lbbrown.com ❈ clewis1942@yahoo.com

Program for L. B. Brown Heritage Festival in 2012

Great Floridian 2000

The Florida Department of State and the Florida League of Cities created the Great Floridian 2000 program in 1998 to help celebrate the millennium's approaching end. The process dedicated a special series of commemorative panels in cities throughout the state recognizing deceased individuals who made significant contributions to the history and culture of Florida. A total of 385 persons throughout the state subsequently received recognition.

Among them, L. B. Brown was selected as a Great Floridian 2000 as one of the select few who qualified by their lives and achievements as being instrumental in developing Florida.

Great Floridian Plaque mounted on front of Brown House/Museum

Smithsonian Institution

The Smithsonian Institution's National Museum of African American History and Culture in Washington, D.C., was completed and opened in 2016. This half-billion-dollar project honors African American achievements and contributions to our communities and the growth of our nation. It consists of 350,000 square feet of artifacts and stories of the many African American men and women who helped build this nation.

On December 9, 2013, Dr. Deborah Mack, the Smithsonian's Director for Community and Constituent Services visited to accept a foundation stone made by L. B. Brown and bearing his initials. Brown's story and the foundation stone, one of the national museum's inaugural exhibits, is on permanent display in the museum.

Dr. Mack stated that the house itself, its fascinating story notwithstanding, does not attract her as much as L. B. Brown's story. In addition to learning the construction business, he contributed to African-American culture. He boosted the town of Bartow and maintained a spirit of helping those in his community. "Brown is an early historical example of people of talent and a vision and community concern," she declared. "He made a substantial house for himself but he provided that same for those who cannot and many were tenant farmers and freed slaves." (The Polk County Democrat, November 27, 2013)

La Fleur Paysour, spokeswoman for the museum, underscored the significance of the foundation stone and L. B. Brown's story. "What makes this story so unique is the fact that the home he built is still standing and it includes artifacts that he made himself," she detailed. "That allows us to tell the story through those items, and to encourage people to leave our museum and go right to Bartow and see the house itself."

She continued: "It's rare to find a home that was built in the late 1800s, and is still able to tell the story in the elements of architecture and the things that were inside the house. The man himself is worthy of attention because he is resilience and entrepreneurship personified. He was a self-taught craftsman who built things for his community, and to have those things still in existence, we are fortunate to have that story."

FROM SLAVERY TO COMMUNITY BUILDER

Celebrating the uncelebrated

Brown house, life to be featured at Smithsonian

By JEFF ROSLOW
JROSLOW@HEARTLANDNEWSPAPERS.COM

A bit of Bartow is going to Washington.

Specifically it's the L.B. Brown House. When the African-American Museum opens in 2015 at the Smithsonian Institution pictures of the house and the life of the L.B. Brown, the freed slave who built up much of that section of Bartow will be on display there.

And what that means for the area is exciting, said Cliff Lewis, the president of the Neighborhood Improvement Committee.

"It's not for our sake, but for the area's sake," Lewis said

HOUSE | 5

Cliff Lewis, right, talks about L.B. Brown's willingness to work across racial lines and how he helped the community in Bartow while Deborah L. Mack, director of Community and Constituent Services for the Smithsonian, listens. The Brown House and his legacy will be featured at the museum's African-American Museum which will is scheduled to open in November 2015. Here they were sitting in a living room in the Brown House and with them was also LaFleur Paysour with the Smithsonian and Bartow resident Chuck Warren.

Clifton Lewis talking with Deborah Mack, Director of Community and Constituent Services for the Smithsonian

The L. B. Brown exhibit at the Smithsonian Institute's National Museum of African American History and Culture.

City of Bartow Street Named after L. B. Brown

In recognizing the importance of Mr. Brown to the community, the City of Bartow named a street after him: L. B. Brown Avenue now runs in front of the L.B. Brown House Museum.

University of South Florida College of Education

David P. Scott, a Master Teacher Educator at the Gus A. Stavros Center for Free Enterprise and Economic Education at the University of South Florida, learned about L. B. Brown when he heard Clifton Lewis giving a talk on the University of South Florida Public Radio station. He realized that Mr. Brown was a great entrepreneur and an example to this community.

As a result of hearing Mr. Lewis speak, Scott featured L. B. Brown as an outstanding entrepreneur of Polk County in a program that informs high school teachers about Polk County's extraordinary businessmen. The purpose of the program was to enlighten students about free enterprise, financial literacy, and economic education.

L. B. Brown's family is no stranger to education. His son, Clifford Brown, was the principal of Rochelle School and later Vice Principal at Kathleen High School. He was also a football coach. Lorenzo Brown was a teacher and later bedridden with polio. Lovenia taught at Jewett Academy and Union Academy.

On March 12, 2015, twenty-five teachers met at the Brown House to learn about him first-hand. This experience will enrich their teaching of his life and times.

Brown's Living Legacy—The Obstacles

It is remarkable that a person born into slavery and with sparse means could accomplish so much during a time when the barriers against the success of black men were enormous. At the Civil War's end in 1865, four million enslaved persons were freed. Those first days of freedom brought both exhilaration and anxiety for it was unclear what rights former slaves would enjoy, whether they were citizens, and how they would provide for themselves. Although the war over slavery had ended, racism remained to constitute the biggest hurdle for the freedmen and freedwomen to overcome.

Black men and their families faced a host of obstacles. Violence against the black population persisted. In November 1865, oppressive laws called Black Codes suppressed their rights in an attempt to maintain a semblance of the slave system. By their terms, for example, vagrancy laws compelled unemployed black men and women to sign work contracts with a white person. Refusal to sign might lead to an auction at which a white person paid their fine and then forced them to work until fully reimbursed. Not unlike the days of slavery, children could be taken away in the process and placed with white families. No system existed to verify that these children were not being treated abusively.

In 1866 the Ku Klux Klan initiated a brutal reign of violence and repression in Tennessee. Its members perpetrated repeated acts of violence toward black individuals, often targeting those who owned land. In 1871 Congress heard the testimony of many of its victims. As a result, the Enforcement Act enabled the federal government to intervene. Unfortunately, the violence continued and spread through much of the country despite the Klan's decline.

Degradation and ridicule of black people using entertainment, myths, and cultural events became common by the late Nineteenth Century. The effort to portray former slaves and their descendants as second-class citizens played a crucial role in turning the white population against black citizens and their efforts at self-help. White citizens, not wanting to give up power, convinced themselves that any success achieved by black persons would take away from the white population. Falsely portraying black individuals as dumb, incompetent, or lazy made it more palatable to discriminate against them.

Suppression of voting rights for black men, especially in locations where the black population nearly equaled or surpassed the white population became commonplace. Keeping black men from voting ranked as a necessity in order for white men to keep political power. Poll tax payments, reading tests, and other requirements disallowed their voting.

These barriers continued to exist throughout Lawrence Brown's life. Nevertheless, Brown—and numerous other black men and women—used their skills and talents to manage great achievements, found the courage to persevere in spite of dangers, and had the grace to help build their communities and country in spite of the harsh treatment they received. More than enough reasons justify our admiration of them and compels us to be grateful to them.

NOTES

Chapter 1 L. B. Brown Before Bartow

[1] Peter Brown entry, 1870 Federal Census, Gainesville, Florida, Alachua County, p. 369; Rance O. Braley, "Nineteenth Century Archer," 10-12, at https://sites.google.com/site/archerhistoricalsociety/history-of-archer-fl, accessed August 1, 2018; "A Young Hero," *Daily Union* (Washington, DC), June 27, 1856; "Births," L. B. Brown Family Bible, L. B. Brown House and Museum, Bartow (hereafter, Brown Bible.

[2] Braley, "Nineteenth Century Archer," 12-13; "Atlantic and Gulf Railroad," *Times-Picayune* (New Orleans, La.), June 23, 1859; *Floridian and Journal* (Tallahassee, Fla.), July 30, 1859, p. 2; "Death of James T. Archer," *Savannah Morning News* (Savannah, Ga.), June 7, 1859; "The Florida Rail Road," *Charleston Courier* (Charleston, SC), June 19, 1860.

[3] Braley, "Nineteenth Century Archer," 13-14.

[4] William Watson Davis, *The Civil War and Reconstruction in Florida* (reprint ed., Gainesville: University of Florida Press, 1964), 152-53, 305; David J. Coles, "Far from Fields of Glory: Military Operations in Florida during the Civil War, 1864-1865" (Ph. D. dissertation, Florida State University, 1996), 233-39; Braley, "Nineteenth Century Archer," 14-15.

[5] Peter Brown entry, 1870 Federal Census, Gainesville, Florida, Alachua County, p. 369; Larry Eugene Rivers, *Slavery in Florida, Territorial Days to Emancipation* (Gainesville: University Press of Florida, 2000), 106; Brown family materials, L. B. Brown House and Museum; Braley, "Nineteenth Century Archer," 14; *Minutes of the Annual Conferences of the Methodist Episcopal Church, South, for the Year 1867* (Nashville, Tenn.: Southern Methodist Publishing House, 1870), 126-27.

[6] Rivers, *Slavery in Florida*, 247-48; Larry Eugene Rivers and Canter Brown, Jr., *Laborers in the Vineyard of the Lord: The Beginnings of the AME Church in Florida, 1865-1895* (Gainesville: University Press of Florida, 2001), 12-17; *Minutes of the Annual Conferences of the Methodist Episcopal Church*

for the Year 1868 (New York: Carlton and Lanahan, no date), 11-12; *Minutes of the Annual Conferences of the Methodist Episcopal Church for the Year 1869* (New York: Carlton and Lanahan, no date), 126-27; *Minutes of the Annual Conferences of the Methodist Episcopal Church for the Year 1870* (New York: Carlton and Lanahan, no date), 9-10.

[7]"S. Carolina Conf. Appointments," *Methodist Advocate* (Atlanta, Ga.), February 2, 1870; Luther P. Jackson, "The Educational Efforts of the Freedmen's Bureau and Freedmen's Aid Societies in South Carolina, 1862-1872," *Journal of Negro History* 8 (January 1923), 38; "And Still Another," *Christian Recorder* (Philadelphia, Pa.), May 29, 1873; Marriage Licenses, Vol. A (1869-1878), 125, Alachua County Courthouse, Gainesville, Fla.

[8]"Mt. Pisgah Methodist Episcopal Church," Archer, Florida, in WPA Church Records, State Library of Florida, Tallahassee (hereafter, Church Records); "Testimony Taken before the Special Committee on Investigation of the Election in Florida, Appointed under Resolution of the House of Representatives, Forty-fourth Congress, December 4, 1876," House Misc. Doc. 35, Part 1, 44th Congress, 2d Session (Washington: Government Printing Office, 1877), 275; Brown family materials, L. B. Brown House Museum; Canter Brown, Jr., *Florida's Black Public Officials, 1867-1924* (Tuscaloosa: University of Alabama Press, 1998), 105-106; Rivers and Brown, *Laborers in the Vineyard of the Lord*, 53-54, 57-58, 66, 68-72, 76, 83-85, 101.

[9]"From Florida," *Christian Recorder* (Philadelphia, Pa.), April 15, 1871; Rivers and Brown, *Laborers in the Vineyard of the Lord*, 71-72.

[10]"Florida Correspondence," *Christian Recorder* (Philadelphia, Pa.), June 10, 1871.

[11]Brown, *Florida's Black Public Officials*, 1-21, 135; Davis, *Civil War and Reconstruction in Florida*, 427; Rivers and Brown, *Laborers in the Vineyard of the Lord*, 50-71. On Josiah T. Walls, see Peter D. Klingman, *Josiah Walls: Florida's Black Congressman of Reconstruction* (Gainesville: University of Florida Press, 1976).

[12]Peter Brown entries, Alachua County, Florida, tax rolls, 1867-1878 (available on microfilm, Florida Archives, Tallahassee); Brown, *Florida's Black Public Officials*, 16, 19; Rivers and Brown, *Laborers in the Vineyard of the Lord*, 57-58.

[13]"Letter from Florida," *Savannah Morning News* (Savannah, Ga.), May 10, 1872.

[14]Jerrell H. Shofner, *Nor Is It Over Yet: Florida in the Era of Reconstruction, 1863-1877* (Gainesville: University of Florida Press, 1974), 51-56; "Beauties of the Ballot in Florida," *Savannah Morning News*, November 18, 1874.

[15]*Florida Election, 1876: Report of the Senate Committee on Privileges and Elections, with the Testimony and Documentary Evidence, on the Election in the State of Florida in 1876* (Washington, DC: Government Printing Office, 1877), 86.

[16]Shofner, *Nor Is It Over Yet*, 312-39; *Florida Election, 1876*, 134, 136.

[17]*Florida Election, 1876*, 134.

[18]Judgment Record C, 542, Alachua County Clerk of Court, Gainesville; "From Jacksonville," *Savannah Morning News* (Savannah, Ga.), April 24, 1878.

[19]"Florida," *Chicago Tribune* (Chicago, Ill.), February 14, 1881.

[20]"The Backbone of Volusia County, Fla.--Spring Garden," *Savannah Morning News* (Savannah, Ga.), March 26, 1878; "A Winter in Florida," *Inter Ocean* (Chicago, Ill.), March 24, 1877; "Chicago in Florida," *Chicago Tribune* (Chicago, Ill.), April 9, 1879; ibid., "Notes and News," March 26, 1878.

[21]"Florida" and "Chicago in Florida," *Chicago Tribune*, September 14, 1872, April 9, 1879; "Florida Affairs" and "Backbone of Volusia County, Fla.--Spring Garden ," *Savannah Morning News*, March 16, 1877, March 26, 1878; "A Winter in Florida," *Inter Ocean* (Chicago, Ill.), March 24, 1877; "Florida Correspondence," *Racine Journal* (Racine, Wi.), April 17, 1878; George M. Barbour, *Florida for Tourists, Invalids, and Settlers* (New York: D. Appleton and Company, 1884), 41-43; Spring Garden, Volusia County, Florida, in Record of Appointment of Postmasters, 1832-1971, M841, roll 42, National Archives, Washington, DC.

[22]Lawrence Brown, Benjamin B. Debbin, and Charles Delano entries, 1880 Federal census, 2nd District, Volusia County, Florida, p. 18; Spring Garden, Volusia County, Florida, in Record of Appointment of Postmasters, 1832-1971; "The Bar of DeLand," *Florida Agriculturalist* (DeLand, Fla.), January 17, 1906; "Uriah Mitchell Bennett Called to Last Reward," *Miami News* (Miami, Fla.), July 13, 1918.

[23]L. B. Brown and B. B. Brown entries, 1885 state census, Spring Garden, Florida, Volusia, County, p. 44; Marriage License Records, 1857-1913, Book 2B, 119; Volusia County Records Maintenance Center, DeLand, Fla.; Brown Family Bible and Lawrence B. Brown deed record notes, L. B. Brown

House and Museum; "Notes of Travel in Florida No. 46," *Otsego Farmer* (Cooperstown, NY), January 1, 1887; "St. Johns Missionary Baptist Church," Glenwood, Volusia County, in Church Records.

[24] "A Good Nomination," *Ottawa Free Trader* (Ottawa, Ill.), July 24, 1880; ibid., February 12, 1881, p. 4.

[25] *Laws of Florida* (1881), 139-42; *Ottawa Free Trader* (Ottawa, Ill.), February 12, 1881, p. 4.

[26] "Sunny South" and "Silver Wedding," *Ottawa Free Trader* (Ottawa, Ill.), May 13, 1882, June 19, 1886; "A Negro Exodus," *New York Times*, January 19, 1884; *Palatka Daily News* (Palatka, Fla.), March 13, 1884, p. 5; "St. Johns Missionary Baptist Church" and "Mount Olive African Methodist Episcopal Church, Glenwood, Volusia County, in Church Records; Charles Delano, L. B. Brown, and B. B. Brown entries, 1885 state census, Spring Garden, Florida, Volusia, County, p. 44.

[27] "Notes of Travel in Florida No. 46," *Otsego Farmer* (Cooperstown, NY), January 1, 1887; "A Florida Homestead Free," *Hagerstown Exponent* (Hagerstown, Ind.), December 15, 1886.

[28] Lawrence B. Brown deed record notes, L. B. Brown House and Museum.

[29] Ibid., Brown Family Bible and Brown family materials.

[30] Canter Brown, Jr., *In the Midst of All That Makes Life Worth Living: Polk County, Florida, to 1940* (Tallahassee: Sentry Press, 2001), 93-94, 142-44; ibid., *"Bartow in the place for our people to go": Race and the Course of Life in Southern Polk County, 1865-1905* (Bartow, Fla.: Polk County Historical Association, no date), 9-11.

[31] "Key West (Fla.) Notes," *Star of Zion* (Salisbury, NC), March 21, 1889.

[32] "Elected to the Florida Legislature," *Buffalo Commercial* (Buffalo, NY), December 9, 1886; "Qui Bono," *Pensacolian* (Pensacola, Fla.), August 4, 1888; "Obituary Notes," *World* (New York, NY), October 11, 1890; Brown, *Florida's Black Public Officials*, 63-69; Peter D. Klingman, *Neither Dies Nor Surrenders: A History of the Republican Party in Florida, 1867-1970* (Gainesville: University of Florida Press, 1984), 98-195.

[33] "A Great Fruit-Grower Gone" and "Deaths," *Chicago Tribune* (Chicago, Ill.), December 18, 1887, September 21, 1890; "Obituary Notes," *World* (New York, NY), October 11, 1890; "Hon. Isaac Stone," *Boston Herald* (Boston, Mass.), October 9, 1890; "Quicker Time to Key West," *Daily Glean-*

er (Kingston, Jam.), July 20, 1892; "Will of Charles Delano," Volusia County, Florida, Will Records, Book D (1874-1901), 157-58.

³⁴Brown, *In the Midst of All That Makes Life Worth Living*, 179-80; Brown family materials, L. B. Brown House and Museum.

Chapter 2 Lawrence Brown's Life in Bartow

¹"Historic Properties Survey of the City of Bartow, Florida," by Historic Property Associates, Inc., St. Augustine, Florida 32085, December 1991 p. 9

²"Historic Properties Survey of the City of Bartow, Florida," by Historic Property Associates, Inc., St. Augustine, Florida 32085, December 1991, Continuation Sheet Section 8, p. 3.

³Brown, Canter, Jr., In the Midst of All That Makes Life Worth Living Polk County, Florida, to 1940, Sentry Press, Tallahassee, FL, 2001, p. 190.

⁴Brown, Canter, Jr., In the Midst of All That Makes Life Worth Living Polk County, Florida, to 1940, Sentry Press, Tallahassee, FL, 2001, p. 203.

⁵Materials in the L. B. Brown House Museum archives.

⁶Johnston, Sidney, National Register of Historic Places Continuation sheet Section 8, Page 2. Located in LB Brown House Museum archives.

⁷Lewis, Clifton, Notes in LB Brown House Museum Archives

⁸Johnston, Sidney, National Register of Historic Places Continuation sheet Section 8, Page 3. Located in LB Brown House Museum archives.

⁹Clifton, Lewis, notes to author

¹⁰Thomas, Lovinia Brown, in her essay Historical Facts About My Paternal and Maternal Grassroots, in LB Brown House Museum Archives.

¹¹From "Historic Properties Survey of the City of Bartow, Florida," by Historic Property Associates, Inc., St. Augustine, Florida 32085, December 1991, p. 9.

[12] Brown, Jr., Canter, A Frosty Gilded Age, 1886-1895 in *In the Midst of all that Makes Life Worth Living Polk County, Florida, to 1940* (Tallahassee: Sentry Press, 2001), 167

[13] Burton, LaFrancine K., "Bartow Led Education of Polk's Black Children, Beginning About 1880" The Ledger, Saturday, July 12, 2003, A15

[14] Ibid

[15] Hetherington, M. F., History of Polk County Florida, The Record Company, St. Augustine FL 1928, p 39-73.

[16] Brown, Jr., Canter, "Race and the Course of Life in Southern Polk County, 1865-1905," 14.

[17] Brown, Jr., Canter, "Race and the Course of Life in Southern Polk County, 1865-1905," 15.

[18] Canter Brown, Jr., *In the Midst of All That Makes Life Worth Living Polk County, Florida, to 1940*, 2001, Chapter 10, "As the Century Turned, 1895-1906," page 203

[19] Brown, Jr., Canter, "Race and the Course of Life in Southern Polk County, 1865-1905," 16-17.

[20] Hetherington, M. F., History of Polk County Florida, The Record Company, St. Augustine FL 1928, p. 56

[21] Canter Brown, Jr., *In the Midst of All That Makes Life Worth Living Polk County, Florida, to 1940*, 2001, Chapter 11, "Seasons Before the Storm, 1906-1914," p. 226.

[22] Canter Brown, Jr., *In the Midst of All That Makes Life Worth Living Polk County, Florida, to 1940*, 2001, Chapter 10, "As the Century Turned, 1895-1906" p. 192.

[23] Ibid.

[24] Canter Brown, Jr., *In the Midst of All That Makes Life Worth Living Polk County, Florida, to 1940*, 2001, Chapter 10, "As the Century Turned, 1895-1906" p. 198,199.

[25] Ibid. P. 206.

[26] Ibid. p. 207.

[27]Canter Brown, Jr., *In the Midst of All That Makes Life Worth Living Polk County, Florida, to 1940*, 2001, Chapter 11, "Seasons Before the Storm, 1906-1914" p. 211, 212.

[28]Hetherington, M. F., History of Polk County Florida, The Record Company, St. Augustine FL 1928, p. 56.

[29]Hetherington, M. F., History of Polk County Florida, The Record Company, St. Augustine FL 1928, p. 57.

[30]Canter Brown, Jr., *In the Midst of All That Makes Life Worth Living Polk County, Florida, to 1940*, 2001, Chapter 11, "Seasons Before the Storm, 1906-1914" p. 229.

[31]Hetherington, M. F., History of Polk County Florida, The Record Company, St. Augustine FL 1928, p. 58.

[32]Hetherington, M. F., History of Polk County Florida, The Record Company, St. Augustine FL 1928, p. 61.

[33]Canter Brown, Jr., *In the Midst of All That Makes Life Worth Living Polk County, Florida, to 1940*, 2001, Chapter 11, "Seasons Before the Storm, 1906-1914" p. 228.

[34]Canter Brown, Jr., *In the Midst of All That Makes Life Worth Living Polk County, Florida, to 1940*, 2001, Chapter 12, "The Time of the Great War, 1914-1919," pp. 235-243.

[35]From "Historic Properties Survey of the City of Bartow, Florida," by Historic Property Associates, Inc., St. Augustine, Florida 32085, December 1991, p. 10.

[36]Canter Brown, Jr., *In the Midst of All That Makes Life Worth Living Polk County, Florida, to 1940*, 2001, Chapter 12, "The Time of the Great War, 1914-1919," pp. 245-254.

[37]Canter Brown, Jr., *In the Midst of All That Makes Life Worth Living Polk County, Florida, to 1940*, 2001, "A Patriotic Boom, 1919-1926," pp. 256-259.

[38]McMullen, Cary from an article in the Lakeland Ledger written during Black History Month (no date on the article.)

[39]Wikipedia

[40] From "Historic Properties Survey of the City of Bartow, Florida," by Historic Property Associates, Inc., St. Augustine, Florida 32085, December 1991, p. 12

[41] Canter Brown, Jr., *In the Midst of All That Makes Life Worth Living Polk County, Florida, to 1940*, 2001, "A Patriotic Boom, 1919-1926," pp. 265-269.

[42] Canter Brown, Jr., *In the Midst of All That Makes Life Worth Living Polk County, Florida, to 1940*, 2001, Chapter 14, "The Bust, 1926-1933," pp. 290-293.

[43] Canter Brown, Jr., *In the Midst of All That Makes Life Worth Living Polk County, Florida, to 1940*, 2001, Chapter 14, "The Bust, 1926-1933," pp. 293-294.

[44] From "Historic Properties Survey of the City of Bartow, Florida," by Historic Property Associates, Inc., St. Augustine, Florida 32085, December 1991, p. 9

[45] Canter Brown, Jr., *In the Midst of All That Makes Life Worth Living Polk County, Florida, to 1940*, 2001, Chapter 15, "The Great Depression, 1933-1940," pp. 317-324.

Chapter 3 The L. B. Brown House/Museum

1. PC Historical Quarterly March 2005, Vol. 31, No. 4 "Reviving the L.B. Brown Legacy by James V. Holton, Editor

2. **PHQ March 1993 Volume 19 Number 4** "Brown Home is One of Polk's Oldest Historic Homes" by Martha Sawyer This article was published in the Ledger, February 18, 1989.

3. Johnston, Sidney, in a letter to Clifton Lewis dated April 27, 2000.

4. Johnston, Sidney, National Register of Historic Places Continuation Sheet, Section 7, p 1.

INDEX

A

African American Heritage Conference and Festival 77-80; 124-127
African American history 101-102
African Americans on the Tampa Bay Frontier 101
African Methodist Episcopal Church (AME) 4-7; 42
Alachua County martial law 6
African Methodist Episcopal Zion Church (AMEZ) 16, 35-38
American Legion 54
Amusu, The 43
Anders, Lymus A. 4-6
Archer, Florida 2-9

B

Bagwell, Jeff 98
Bassett, Arjancy 21
Bartow: 16, 19-24, 35-39, 42-46, 49-50, 52, 54, 57-62
Bartow Chamber of Commerce 97
Bartow Community Redevelopment Agency 104
Bartow macadam 37
Bartow Memorial Hospital 98
Bear Creek 102
Bennett, Uriah Mitchell 11-12
Bentley, Chuck 97
Billy Bowlegs War 1
Black codes 8, 20, 133

Blue Room 58
Boy Scouts 53
Brewster, Florida 44
Britt, William F. 16, 102
Brittsville 16, 35, 102
Brittsville School 35, 102
Brown, Annie Bell (Burnette) 39-40, 51, 59, 61
Brown, Annie Bell (daughter) 57
Brown, Historian Canter 38, 42, 62, 77, 100-102, 104
Brown, Catherine L. B.'s mother 1, 21, 55
Brown, Clifford 52-53, 132
Brown, Elizabeth Washington 13, 16
Brown, Gilbert marriage 4; death 8
Brown House Museum 73-93, 103-105, 123-124
Brown, L.B: Life before Bartow 1-18, life in Bartow 19-62, 73-74, 111-122, legacy 123-133
Brown, Lorenzo 49, 132
Brown, Louvenia Catherine (spelling of first name varies) 44, 73, 104, 132
Brown, Mary 54, 74
Brown, Peter L. B.'s father 1-9, 15
Brown, Robert 39, 58-59, 61, 74, 88, 104, 116
Burkett Chapple Primitive Baptist Church 42
Burkett, Lela 36, 42
Burkett, Sam 42
Burnette, Benjamin 39-40, 58
Burnette, Thomas Franklin 58

Burt, Jimmie 96
Bush, Willie 96

C
Camp Fire Girls 53
Carolina, Francis B. 4
Census, U. S. 1930 59
Central Florida Regional Planning Council 99
Citrus and Chemical Bank 97
Civil Rights Act: 20
Civil War: 3-4, 20
Clara Frye Hospital 40, 59
Clark, Ella 38
Clark, Mayme (Burden) 97
Colored Red Cross Society 54
Community Development Block Grant 82, 99
Constitution, U. S. 20, 56-57
Courier-Informant 36, 45-46
"Crackers" 10

D
Darwin, Charles 57
Davis, Isaac 6
Debbin, Benjamin B. association with Lawrence Brown 11, 13
Deer Hammock 1
Delano, Charles 11, 13, 17
DeLegge, Joseph 97, 99, 103
DeLeon Springs 10-12, 14, 15, 23
Democrats 7, 9, 16
Denham, James M. "Mike" 77, 100, 101, 102, 104
DeSoto Springs Hotel 14
Dixon, Stepney 102

E
Earnest, Charles 57
Edward Waters College 43
Enforcement Act 133

F
First Presbyterian Church 97
First Providence Missionary Baptist Church 16, 35, 96, 102
Fitzgerald, Scott 56
Flager, Henry 15
Florida A&M College 43
Florida Bureau of Historical Resources 104
Florida Constitution: Congressional or military reconstruction 6
Florida Normal and Industrial School (Florida Memorial) 44
Florida State Division of Historical Preservation 104

G
Gainesville AME Church laying of cornerstone 6
General election 1874 8
Graham, State Senator Ernest 60
Granger, George and Lenora 39
Great Depression 60
Great Floridian 2000 128
Great Freeze 35, 38
Green, Ned 35

H
Haircut agreement 33
Hallie Mae 21
Harris, George 97
Harris, Lloyd 61
Hatch, Reverend Jim 97, 98
Hillsborough County 60
Hoch, Jeffery 98
Holland, State Senator Spessard 60
Holland and Knight Law Firm 97

J

Jim Crow Laws 20, 38
Johnson, Clarence C. 35, 46
Johnson, Prince 35, 102
Johnson, W. H. 38
Johnston, Sidney 74-75
Jones, Loraine 104
Journals (Ledgers) 22-34, 41, 46-51

K

Keystone Challenge Fund 98
Knight, Ben 25-32
Ku Klux Klan 57, 133

L

L. B. Brown Avenue 21, 132
Landers general election 1874 8
Laurent, John 103
Leonard, Doug 99
Leonard, Mabel 96
Lewis, Clifton 61, 77, 95, 96, 97, 100, 104, 113, 132
Lomax, Bishop T. H. 36
Long, Elder Thomas Warren 5
Longworth, Jack C. 15, 35
Lynching 38, 39, 60

M

Mack, Dr. Deborah 129
Macon, Charles Henry 35, 45
Marquis, T. L. 43
Martial law 6
Martin, Charles 43
Mathews, Tom 98
Mays, George H. Jr. 54
McKinney Creek 102
McNeill, Charlie 58
McNeill, Dr. Ledge Wynn 54, 58

Methodist Episcopal Church, South: 4
Milam, Louis N. 20-21, 24-25, 32-33, 36
Moore, Andy 35, 102
Moore, Tanner Reid 102
Mount Olive AME Church 14
Mt. Gilboa Missionary Baptist Church 21-22, 58, 62
Mt. Pisgah 5-6
Mt. Zion A. M. E. Church 61
Murphy, John 104
Murray, C. E. 46
Myrick, Willie Jr. 96

N

NAACP 42
National Register of Historic Places 74, 77, 124
Neighborhood Improvement Corporation of Bartow (NIC) 95-104
New Deal 60
Nico, Myrtice 96
Norris, A. Hart 14
Norris, George H. 10-16

O

Obstacles to Brown's Success 25, 133
Over the Branch 102

P

Pasco County 1
Paysour, La Fleur 129
Peninsular Telephone Company 38, 42
Phosphate 19, 31, 37, 39, 43, 52, 54-55, 58, 61, 101, 123
Polk County Historical Association 103
Polk County Record 62
Polk County Woodturners 104
Poll tax 16, 20, 54, 60, 133
Port Royal, South Carolina 4

Providence Baptist 16, 35-36
Public school 5, 6, 44, 57, 102
Putnam, Adam 103

R

Race relations 20, 36, 38-39, 42, 45-46, 53-54, 57, 60, 101
Railroad 1-3, 10, 12-17, 19, 21, 37, 52, 58, 61, 77
Red Cross 53, 54
Reese, Albert 97, 98
Religion 4
Rental House 93
Republicans 8, 9, 10, 16
Rivers, Larry Eugene 4, 77
Robinson Funeral Parlor 58
Rochelle, Fred 38
Roosevelt, President Franklin 60

S

Scarborough, Charles 42
Scott, Frank 42
Selective Service Act 53
Separate but equal doctrine 20
Shaw University 44
Sheets, Sandy 97
Smart Set Club 43
Smithsonian Institution's National Museum of African American History and Culture 129-130
Spanish Influenza 54
Spring Garden 9-17
St. James AME 16, 36, 38
St. Johns Missionary Baptist Church 12
Star of Zion AMEZ Church 38
Stone, Isaac 14, 16-17
Strong, Gwen 96
Summerlin Institute 35
Sunday, Billy 54
Sweet, Henry and Dora L. 43

Sweet, William DeVaughn 43
Sweet, Ossian 43

T

Taggert, Rena 38
The Golden Way to the Highest Attainments 111-122
Third Seminole War 1
Thomas, Robert 44
Tillis, Dallas 38
Tugerson, Joseph 54
Tuskegee Institute 54

U

Union Academy 36, 44, 54, 102, 132
University of South Florida 132

V

Victor Boys and Girls 53
Victory Gardens 53

W

Wacahoota 1, 9
Waldon, Fred 35, 58
Waldon, Thomas 102
Walker, C. H. 42
Walls, Josiah T. 6
Watson, Geraldine 98
Welch, Rev. Jackson 4
West Bartow 35, 38, 95-103
West Bartow Improvement Committee 96, 97
Williams, Ben 96
Williams, Reverend Earl Brown 96, 98
Winter Haven Woodcrafters 104
World War I 53-54
World War II 52, 61
Wright, Freddie 103

www.ingramcontent.com/pod-product-compliance
Lightning Source LLC
Chambersburg PA
CBHW051211290426
44109CB00021B/2413